GARDENS
ILLUSTRATED

PLANT
PROFILES

GARDENS
ILLUSTRATED

PLANT
PROFILES

EDITED BY ROSIE ATKINS

BBC

CONTENTS

Introduction

Gardens Illustrated magazine launched in 1993 and, in every reader's survey since, the 'Plant Profiles' have been rated the most widely read and most appreciated section of the magazine. Now the magazine is celebrating its tenth anniversary it seems obvious to collect the best of these features, which are a heady mix of expert knowledge and stunning photography, into a book.

My first task when launching this international magazine was to seduce the reader into making the connection between plants, places and people. Gardeners had become tired of reading repetitive, second-hand stories and advice and craved stimulating, entertaining information on all aspects of gardening and in particular on plants.

The magazine has gone on to win many awards and I am sure under its current Editor, Clare Foster, it will continue to be a benchmark for good journalism and ground-breaking graphic design. The magazine has been lucky to attract talented staff but I should also acknowledge the contribution of publishers John Brown and now BBC Worldwide, who have supported and believed in the title. We also have the benefit of three marvellous Associate Editors, Anna Pavord, Penelope Hobhouse and Dan Pearson. This triumvirate continue to be a combination of godparents and ambassadors for the magazine, not to mention contributing some memorable articles. They all helped develop the philosophy of the magazine and, after each magazine has hit the newsstands, the Associate Editors meet with the editorial staff to give their appraisal of the issue. Having such discerning critics has always made us strive to surprise and excite our readers.

All the Associate Editors agree that the 'Plant Profiles' are the heartbeat of the magazine. Dan Pearson, the world-renowned garden designer and plantsman, has always held plants dear to his heart. "What I love about the 'Plant Profiles' in Gardens Illustrated is they explore a group of plants in real depth. These pieces give you all the 'ins and outs' of a genus so you have the confidence to experiment with a plant you may not have thought about growing before. This sharing of hard-won knowledge and first-hand experiences of handling specific plants is a rare and valuable thing."

Penelope Hobhouse, garden historian and doyenne of international garden design, is always ready to re-evaluate a family of plants. She understands how plants can prompt you to reinvent your garden design and planting style. "The 'Plant Profiles' have always been the first thing I turn to when my copy of *Gardens Illustrated* arrives," Penny enthuses. "I also enjoy reading about plants such as sarracenias, which I know I am not going to grow, and the images are always excellent. I cannot wait to have all these profiles together in one book."

Anna Pavord's name is now synonymous with tulips, since the publication of her bestselling book, *The Tulip* (1999). She currently chairs the Garden Panel of the National Trust and her columns in the *Independent* are required reading for all keen gardeners. "British gardeners are essentially plantaholics," she says. "We often get into gardening through plants that we scoop up without really thinking about what to do with them. Falling in love with plants is a wonderfully sympathetic way to garden, but you get to a point where you want to learn a bit more about them. The strength of *Gardens Illustrated* has always been the quality of its illustrations and the 'Plant Profiles' have always been illustrated in a bold and lavish way. So much so, you really want to pick the plants off the page. This, coupled with the fact the person who has written the piece is the font of all wisdom on that genus, means you are really getting to the heart of the subject."

The following chapters include profiles of 25 plants and genera. We have grouped them into plants with similar characteristics — for example, the spring flowers can be found in 'Early Risers', in 'Show Stoppers' you will find some perennials whose form provides a lot of impact in the garden and in 'Strong Performers' are collected some robust plants that will survive the worst winters. The writers of the profiles were chosen because of their intimate knowledge of those plants. They may be National Collection holders, or they may even have identified new species in the wild, but they have all grown and studied these plants with unique dedication. They explain the provenance of the plant and what other plants it likes to associate with, cover the historical significance and provide hands-on instructions for propagation and cultivation. The results often read like a good novel.

You will find nurserymen, such as John Hoyland, Alan Street or Joe Sharman, and plant collectors, such as Jamie Compton, Brian Mathew and Martyn Rix. Other contributors, for example, Rupert Bowlby and John Vanderplank, even are both. Beth Chatto, the gardening guru, contributed the profile on fritillaries for the very first issue of *Gardens Illustrated*. From her first sentence you can tell she has a real affection for her subject: 'Except for the large and well-known crown imperial, *Fritillaria imperialis*, most fritillaries do not flaunt themselves from yards away and do not contribute overtly to the overall design of a border; yet, for many enthusiasts, they are irresistible.' Then there are the new 'Young Turks of the gardening world', such as Alasdair Moore. His piece on proteas conveys pure infectious enthusiasm as well as a unique insight into how these extraordinary plants are able to survive 100-mile-per-hour winds, laden with salt, in their native African Cape and thrive on the island of Tresco where he gardens.

But what really makes you want to know more about an unfamiliar group of plants is the way they look and ultimately whether they appeal to you. Photographers, such as Howard Sooley, like nothing better than focusing their cameras on a plant and making you look twice. Remember his pictures in that wonderful book on Derek Jarman's seaside garden? When Howard's pictures of proteas and arisaemas came into the *Gardens Illustrated*

OPPOSITE: *PASSIFLORA 'PURA VIDA'.*

office the art department were unable to contain their astonishment. The images used in the 'Plant Profiles' make it hard not to want to find out more.

As artist turned journalist, getting to the heart of a subject has always held a great appeal for me. In March 2002 I was lured from *Gardens Illustrated* by the prospect of becoming Curator of Chelsea Physic Garden in London, founded by the Worshipful Society of Apothecaries in 1673. Suddenly it is real plants not photographs and gardeners not writers that fill my day, although I hope the writing will never stop. We have over 5,000 taxa in our 3.8 acres of hallowed ground, preserved in a deed of covenant drawn up by our benefactor, Sir Hans Sloane (1660–1753). Sloane was a friend of Isaac Newton and Christopher Wren, physician to the royal family and collector of natural curiosities that formed the nucleus of The British Museum. He studied the healing arts as an apprentice apothecary at Chelsea Physic Garden at a time when knowing the difference between a pulmonaria and a primula could be a matter of life and death.

Sloane described Chelsea Physic Garden as a garden dedicated to the study of useful plants and there is no better place to ponder the beauty and importance of plants. Sadly we no longer go on herborising expeditions up the River Thames on a gaily painted barge like the apothecaries. But walking through the systematic beds, which are a living version of 'Plant Profiles', you can spot the family resemblance among the different species in each genus. It excites me to think Dr James Compton, who was Head Gardener at Chelsea Physic Garden from 1984–1990, is now Botanical Advisor on *Gardens Illustrated*. James is unusual in that he is able to identify plants portrayed in photographs and examine their DNA under a microscope; he also travels the world to find new species. Sadly there aren't enough scientists like Dr Compton around today. The current trend is for botanists to concentrate on molecular biology rather than taxonomy, which will no doubt cause problems in the future, certainly when it comes to finding staff to work in botanic gardens who are able to identify one plant from another.

Plant identification was certainly important to Philip Miller, Curator at Chelsea Physic Garden from 1722–1771 and one of the most influential gardeners in British history. He published a succession of dictionaries on plants that were updated on a regular basis to encompass new discoveries and the latest scientific theories. The Swedish botanist, Carl Linnaeus, who formalised the use of the binomial system of nomenclature (using one word to describe the genus and another to describe the species), visited the Chelsea Physic Garden in 1738. It took a while for Miller to accept the new system but he eventually embraced it wholeheartedly. Sadly, Philip Miller left the garden in disgrace after a dispute over cataloguing plants. Having lived for the garden for 50 years he died a few months after his departure. What passions plants evoke.

A dear friend gave me a copy of one of Philip Miller's bestselling publications, *The Gardener's Kalendar*, dated 1762. This precious book makes excellent reading even today. In his introduction Miller says, 'All the sciences have their proper language but Botany alone has almost as many different languages as there are different authors.' Miller was a master of making plants more accessible to people. I believe the 'Plant Profiles' gathered in this volume do the same. I hope you agree.

Rosie Atkins, 2003

OPPOSITE: *EUCOMIS PALLIDIFLORA* **AND** *LILIUM SPECIOSUM VAR. RUBRUM.*

EARLY RISERS

Fritillaries

Except for the large and well-known crown imperial, *Fritillaria imperialis*, most fritillaries do not flaunt themselves from yards away and do not contribute overtly to the overall design of a border; yet, for many enthusiasts, they are irresistible. Dancing waves of daffodils may be soul-stirring but, come spring time, it is the fritillaries I am looking for in my garden. Many species grow wild in temperate regions all around the globe, in such varying conditions as cool woodlands, open meadows or bare rocky mountain slopes. They have an almost hypnotic appeal, with nodding, bell-shaped flowers on slender stems in curiously subtle shades and colours – mysterious flowers of early spring.

Perhaps the earliest introduction was the flamboyant crown imperial, who can trace her ancestry back, according to legend, to the days when she refused to bow her head as Christ passed by on the way to Calvary. From that time on, her haughty head has been bowed in shame,

with unshed tears concealed in every flower, nature's design to attract pollinating insects with sweet pools of nectar. As early as 1611, John Tradescant was writing an account for the first Earl of Salisbury of 'fortye fritillarias at three pence a peece' from Holland. By the end of the 18th century there was a vast choice in cultivation and the favourites were frequently mentioned in verse and studied in flower painting. As early as 1620, an Amsterdam goldsmith, Daniel von Pilcom, fashioned in gold a replica of a flower of *F. meleagris*, which opened to reveal a miniature watch. This exquisite piece of work can be seen in The British Museum in London.

In my garden, some time in early spring, a particularly pungent scent wafted on a soft wind makes me aware of the presence of *F. imperialis*, long before I've noticed the first fat buds pushing through the bare earth. Some people find it distasteful, a foxy smell they say, but I find it exciting, one of the earliest signals to tell me that the

PREVIOUS PAGE: *PRIMULA PULVERULENTA.*
OPPOSITE: THE DAINTY YELLOW BELLS OF *FRITILLARIA PALLIDIFLORA* FROM CENTRAL ASIA.

spring garden is coming to life. The thick stems, clothed in whorls of juicy green leaves, burst through the cold soil with amazing speed, soon to be topped with a corona of lemon-yellow or burnt orange bells beneath a pineapple-like tuft of leaves.

Fritillaria persica, from southern Turkey, Iraq and Israel, grows on warm rocky slopes. It makes a very handsome garden plant in warmer countries, in well drained, well fed soil. Standing about 75cm (2½ft) tall, it carries tapering heads of dusky purple, grape-coloured bells clustered close to the stems above whorls of grey-green leaves. *F. persica* 'Adiyaman' is a fine selected form, taller and more floriferous. Plants such as the silvery-grey artemisias or santolinas make a good background for these fritillaries.

In my Essex garden I grow outdoors only those fritillaries that flower well and multiply provided I choose

ABOVE LEFT: A MASS OF *F. GRAECA*. **ABOVE RIGHT: THE UNUSUAL BLUE-BLACK BELLS OF** *F. TUNTASIA*. **OPPOSITE:** *F. ACMOPETALA*, **FROM CYPRUS AND TURKEY, PRODUCES NARROW, GREEN AND BROWN BLOOMS.**

Morris' collection and is particularly fine.

There is considerable variation in the species. All fritillaries are worth the trouble of bending your back and tipping their faces up to see the often surprising insides.

Another treasure is *F. tuntasia*, a native of Greece, whose small open bells are almost black, enhanced with a silvery sheen, reminding me of ripe sloes.

Although these small fritillaries need suitable companions and settings to show them off, I find I have to cut back invasive sedums or thymes, and surround the bulbs with a mulch of gravel to discourage slugs from chewing them off at ground level. Many forms of sempervivum make suitable companions, as do the silvery, encrusted saxifrages.

Fritillaria acmopetala presents no problems except that it tends to make a lot of tiny bulbs, like grains of rice, around the parent plants. I like the effect of their totally different, large, solitary leaves at ground level, in contrast with the linear, grey leaves that ascend the flowering stems. The long, narrow bells with drawn-in mouths are green and brown, and stand at various levels, some tall, about 60cm (2ft), others shorter, more interesting than all at the same height. I have a drift running through *Libertia peregrinans* whose stiff narrow leaves, almost totally stained orange, make a striking contrast.

For the cooler parts of the garden there are more delights. *Fritillaria pallidiflora* from sub-alpine slopes of the Tien-Shan in Central Asia, is mouth-watering. Several lemon-yellow bells, each about 5cm (2in) long, are held above broad, pale-grey leaves on stems 30–45cm (1–1½ft) tall. In total contrast there is *F. camschatcensis*, which ranges round the northern Pacific, from Japan through Kamschatka and Alaska to British Columbia, growing in moist, open woods. In the garden it likes a cool situation in deep loam with plenty of humus. Sometimes it disappears for a year or more: do not despair, the rest seems to make it more vigorous. In early summer, each flowering

the right conditions. Free-draining gravel soil enriched with compost seems ideal for certain of the Mediterranean species. Average garden soil and full sun would do as well if not better, provided drainage is good. In these conditions, *F. pyrenaica* forms good clumps once established and left in peace. Flowering stems clothed in narrow grey leaves are about 30cm (1ft) tall, each carrying several wide chocolate-brown bells with rolled up edges showing yellowish-green enamelled linings. I think my form may be something special since it came from the late Sir Cedric

ABOVE: THE FROTHY BLOOMS OF *F. IMPERIALIS* 'AUREOMARGINATA'.

stem holds several whorls of shining green leaves, topped with a cluster of open bells. Again I am fortunate to have a good form from Cedric Morris; smooth and matt black on the outside, it is deep mahogany inside with deeply grooved surfaces. This bulb was used as a food plant by North American Indians, boiled and eaten like potatoes.

Another of my favourites, and very effective in the garden, is *F. verticillata*, native to China, and naturalised in Japan, where it is used as a medicinal herb. It forms colonies standing 45–60cm (1½–2ft) tall, the slender stems clothed in very narrow, grey-green leaves, which become curling tendrils towards the top, among spires of delicate drooping bells, cream and green on the outside and pencilled with fine brown chequering within. They flower in early summer, looking lovely above deep blue scillas and low bushes of the dwarf Russian almond, *Prunus tenella*, providing a froth of pink blossom.

Our native member of this exotic family is *F. meleagris*, the aptly-named snake's head fritillary, with wedge-shaped buds opening out to curiously angular shoulders, rather than a rounded top to the bell, a characteristic shared by several other members of the genus. There still remain a few undisturbed water meadows, notably in Suffolk and Oxford, where for a brief magical time they stand in flower as thick as blades of grass.

In my garden, they have slowly increased and seeded in heavy enriched soil, some in cool open borders, others in the grass in open woodland. At Great Dixter, Christopher Lloyd and his mother before him have naturalised them for more than 70 years in an old orchard, on heavy loam. Seedlings produce quite a lot of variation, from white through pale pink, chequered with green, to deep plum chequered with purple.

There are many beautiful species native to the United States, though these are not ones that can be grown outside in British gardens, except by those enthusiasts who grow them successfully in a special environment. They need

much more sunlight and heat, and usually rot in Britain's damp and frequently overcast climate. *Fritillaria affinis* is a very variable western American species, with whorls of narrow leaves and several chequered brown flowers. It's best in a half-shaded bulb frame and kept fairly dry in summer.

Fritillaria recurva is the one we in Britain would all like to grow, from dry hillsides in southern Oregon and California. The scarlet tubular flowers are pollinated by hummingbirds. It needs a bulb frame, or pot in the greenhouse, and to be kept dry in summer.

ABOVE: THE SULPHUR-YELLOW BLOOMS OF *F. IMPERIALIS* 'LUTEA' APPEAR IN EARLY SUMMER.

ABOVE: THE ROBUST SPIRES OF *F. PERSICA* **MAKE A HANDSOME DISPLAY.**
OPPOSITE: *F. IMPERIALIS* 'ORANGE PERFECTION'.

CULTIVATION

While easily grown species, such as *Fritillaria imperialis*, *F. meleagris* and *F. pyrenaica* flower well, and increase in number if left undisturbed, it is advisable, from time to time to lift the bulbs, divide them, and replant in fresh soil or at least in refreshed soil, with liberal additions of well made compost and grit. Blindness (non-flowering bulbs) sometimes results from overcrowding.

It is always worth trying bulbs out in different situations and noting where they appear to do best. Do not wait until a dissatisfied species has deteriorated badly.

PROPAGATION

Fritillary seeds are ready to harvest when they turn brown and dry. Collect them in the autumn when the seed capsule has split open. Prepare a pot with seed compost and sow the seeds on to the surface, then cover the seeds with a fine layer of horticultural grit. Place the pots outside and wait for the seeds to germinate the following spring. Allow the bulbs to grow on for one or two seasons, then during their dormant period in late summer and early autumn, pot them on into larger sized pots. Be patient; it takes between four and six years before the plants reach flowering size.

Fritillaries naturally lend themselves to propagation by division. Some species, like *F. pyrenaica*, produce sizeable offsets, which can be lifted during the dormant period in late summer and early autumn and replanted immediately. Other species, such as *F. recurva*, produce masses of tiny grain-like bulbs, often described as 'rice'. In the dormant period, lift and separate the bulbs and plant them in rows in trays filled with a sandy compost, and grow on using the same technique as described for propagation from seed.

Pulmonarias

Pulmonarias, or lungworts as they are commonly known, are the backbone of the English cottage garden in early spring. There are about 15 species, mostly from western Europe, which usually grow in damp woodland or on stream banks. Grown for their early flowers, which come in a range of pinks, blues and whites, and for their simple, often spotted leaves, they make excellent ground-cover plants for shady areas, looking equally at home among shrubs or woodland plants or at the front of a border. The wind of change is now blowing through the genus, making available many new varieties with different shades of flower colour, and with ever more interesting leaf patterns so choosing between them isn't easy. I can't hope to cover all the plants I have seen and grown over the years but this profile isn't intended to be a comprehensive review – just a personal selection that might give you some ideas about picking the best varieties for your garden.

I have grown pulmonarias for almost as long as I can remember. When I was a gardening-mad teenager, a doting aunt gave me a *Pulmonaria officinalis*, which soon started seeding around and producing interesting things. I also remember growing *P. rubra*, but didn't become totally hooked until after a visit to plantsman Richard Nutt's superb collection in the early 1980s. He generously gave me a starter collection, and I haven't looked back since.

One of the colours most sought after in the spring garden is a lovely rich blue, and this is provided by good forms of the species *P. longifolia* and *P. angustifolia*. The old standby is 'Mawson's Blue', which is still widely grown, but this has been overtaken by the newcomers, the best of which, in my opinion, is 'Blue Ensign' – a vigorous cultivar with rich, dark green leaves, very large, rich blue flowers and a good upright habit. There is little to choose between 'Blauer Hügel', developed by the German nurseryman, Ernst Pagels, and 'Little Star', from Dan Heims in the US.

OPPOSITE: *PULMONARIA 'ROY DAVIDSON',* **AN AMERICAN CULTIVAR WITH SPECTACULARLY SPOTTED LEAVES.**

Both have slightly spotted, long, dark green leaves and produce dense heads of abundant, tubular, rich blue flowers. 'Blaues Meer' is one of the most widely grown European cultivars but it is less well-known in the UK. It has unspotted leaves and is free flowering. 'Blue Crown' was originally selected for its leaves, which have a few large silver spots on dark green, but it is also good in flower. Finally, *P. angustifolia* subsp. *azurea* is widely grown in Britain and has prolific pinky violet to blue flowers.

Now on to the pinks. One of the best pinks is *P. rubra* 'Prestbury Pink', which was found growing in the wild in Czechoslovakia. It is a wonderful sugar-pink but, unfortunately, it is weak and prone to mildew. *P. saccharata* 'Dora Bielefeld' has a vigorous habit, silvery spotted leaves, and many clear pink flowers. This is still the best, in my opinion, although other pinks are being introduced.

There was a time when white-flowered forms usually got lumped under the universal name *P. saccharata* 'Alba'. More and more turned up and were named, but they are still difficult to tell apart. The best form, in my opinion, is 'Oliver Wyatt's White', which has large flowers and very nicely spotted leaves. *Pulmonaria* 'Sissinghurst White' (AGM) comes a close second and is very popular, with pure white flowers and slightly silver-spotted leaves. White forms of *P. rubra* and *P. angustifolia* are also known – *P. rubra* var. *albocorollata* used to be a rarity but is now more widely available. It is pure white and vigorous. *Pulmonaria angustifolia* 'Alba' is a very rare and slowly spreading old cultivar but a well grown plant is wonderful to behold. Both have unspotted leaves.

Of the very pale shades, 'Glacier', vigorous, with green, slightly spotted leaves and large, very pale pink to pale blue flowers, is not yet surpassed. 'Merlin' has narrow, strongly spotted leaves with flowers in a very pale blue. The flowers are small and the plant is not so vigorous, so there is scope for improvement, and this is where 'Ocupol' comes in, vigorous, with larger flowers and well spotted leaves. Of the *P. longifolia* types, the clear winner has to be 'Roy Davidson', an old American cultivar with pale to medium-blue tubular flowers and heavily spotted leaves. *Pulmonaria officinalis* Cambridge Blue Group is another pale form, and very popular – although I sometimes think it is people's affection for the name, rather than the qualities of the plant, that sells it.

Pulmonarias are also grown for their lush green or silver-marked leaves and plants that combine good leaves and flowers are the best to grow. 'Nürnberg' has lovely silver-marked leaves with pink and blue flowers, and somehow seems to combine daintiness with vigour. Completely silver leaves are also possible – the best-known silver-leaved form is *P. saccharata* Argentea Group (AGM) but that can be variable and is now largely superseded. The newer selections have only a narrow green edge to the leaf and have varying degrees of brightness in their silvering. 'Majesté' has large pink to dark blue flowers – the best of the bunch, with 'Cotton Cool' a close second. One of the most desirable but rarely-seen silver-leaved types is *P. longifolia* subsp. *cevennensis*. This has short stems carrying dark blue flowers and the most amazing silver leaves up to 45cm (1½ft) long but only 5cm (2in) wide.

ABOVE: *P. ANGUSTIFOLIA* SUBSP. *AZUREA*.

OPPOSITE: THE POPULAR *P.* 'SISSINGHURST WHITE', **WITH DELICATE PALE FLOWERS AND SILVER-MARKED LEAVES.**

Americans are now waking up to the virtues of *Pulmonaria*. They can't be grown everywhere in the US but they are becoming popular in states with cooler and less extreme climatic conditions, such as Oregon, northern California, and in the northeast. Consequently, a range of American varieties have appeared, but many of them have been named without realising that similar variants have already been named in Britain. Some of the more notable are 'British Sterling' with all-silver leaves on a pale green background which, despite its name, is a new American introduction; 'Berries and Cream', with purpley-pink flowers and the extra character of ruffled leaf edges; and 'Spilled Milk' which has very variably marked leaves with spots, streaks and splashes.

There are now several cultivars with variegated leaves. The first to be successfully launched was *P. rubra* 'David Ward', with white-edged, pale green leaves and brick-pink flowers. However, variegation is not limited merely to leaves and, in the last few years, forms with variegated flowers have been appearing. *Pulmonaria rubra* 'Barfield Pink', for example, has pink and white striped flowers, and

P. rubra 'Ann', superior to 'Barfield Pink', has large, prolific flowers with a spotted leaf. The next big surprise was 'Chintz', introduced in the early 1990s. The very attractive flowers are distinctly striped in blue and white. The plant is not especially vigorous and has mid-green leaves with relatively few silver spots.

Despite all these new plants, we still have several obvious gaps in the possible range of variation. Although a form with purple-tinged leaves has appeared – 'Smoky Blue' – it has poor flowers and is far from ideal. Pulmonarias are in the same family as comfrey and could potentially sport cream, or even yellow flowers. I don't know of any double-flowered forms and there is still plenty of scope for more variegated cultivars.

The decision by the Royal Horticultural Society to hold trials of pulmonaria in their garden at Wisley between 1996 and 1998, focused attention on the genus and brought the new, wider range of varieties to the attention of many more people. Pulmonarias deserve their place in our gardens, and I look forward to more distinct new seedlings and crosses to enhance the selection we already have.

ABOVE LEFT: *P. LONGIFOLIA.* **ABOVE RIGHT: THE WIDELY CULTIVATED** *P. RUBRA.*
OPPOSITE: *P. RUBRA* 'DAVID WARD', **WHICH HAS STRIKING, WHITE-EDGED VARIEGATED LEAVES AND BRICK-PINK FLOWERS.**

ABOVE: DRIFTS OF *P. OFFICINALIS* 'ALBA' THRIVE IN DAPPLED SHADE.
OPPOSITE: *P.* 'BLUE ENSIGN', A VIGOROUS CULTIVAR AND ONE OF THE BEST BLUE-FLOWERING PULMONARIAS.

PROPAGATION

Root cuttings should be taken in autumn. The roots used are usually young strong roots of the current season's growth and are cut into sections of about 5cm (2in) long. These sections are inserted the right way up, into a free-draining compost in cutting trays and overwintered in a cool place. The cultivars and hybrids of *Pulmonaria longifolia* and *P. saccharata* seem to work best with this method. Division works for all species and cultivars. Division in the ground is usually done in autumn or early spring, but for potted plants I have found the best time is midsummer. Top-cuttings can be taken in spring and early summer from new vegetative shoots that appear at the base of the flowering stem either during or just after flowering. Cut off the shoots with a sharp knife, remove the basal leaves, dip them in rooting powder and stick them into sand. Rooting takes place within 3–4 weeks depending on the temperature. Seed should not be used as a method for reproducing cultivars as they will never come exactly true.

CULTIVATION

Cultivation of pulmonarias is easy. They prefer rich, damp soils in part shade but will tolerate a wide variety of conditions provided their summer water needs are met. They can be short-lived, however, and it pays to split up clumps that are beginning to deteriorate. All pulmonarias can be described as hardy but some, notably the rubras, can have their early flowers destroyed by winter frosts. Pulmonaria leaves are susceptible to wind damage, so they should not be planted in exposed positions. Although often described as trouble-free, some pest damage can occur – from caterpillars, aphids, slugs, snails, mildew and eelworm. Mildew is the most disfiguring ailment. It can be lessened, but not prevented, by plenty of air movement and no shortage of water. Badly infected leaves can be removed in autumn and burned to reduce the number of overwintering spores. Several new cultivars claimed to be mildew free have rapidly succumbed! Don't despair, learn to live with it.

Primulas

rimula is one of the largest and most widespread of all genera, with approximately 425 species of mainly herbaceous perennials all distributed throughout the cooler regions of the northern hemisphere. Occurring in a range of habitats from bogs and marshland to mountain areas, most of these species are found in Himalayas and western China. About 100 species can be cultivated in temperate climates such as Britain's and this profile aims to help you select the best garden plants from among them.

On June 26 1936, the eminent British botanist and plant hunter, the late Frank Ludlow, penned in his diary, 'It gave me one of the greatest thrills of my life. On its northern slopes, in a region of incessant rainfall, grew the most amazing variety of plants I have ever seen.' Ludlow was speaking of the Lo La Chu valley in Tibet and one of the plants he was so excited about was the most lovely primula he had ever seen. He named it *Primula elizabethae*

after his mother, yet this was just one of some ten species thriving in this one remarkable valley.

Although Britain's rainfall is relatively low, which means that not all of the wonderful range of primulas thrive, there are many that grow well there. Carolus Linnaeus's naming of the *Primula* genus couldn't be more appropriate – the Latin *primus* means 'first' and the name refers to the early flowering nature of so many of the species. Equally apt would be the word *prima*, suggesting first in importance.

Of the Himalayan species, there are many that can be grown in a temperate climate, though they can sometimes be a challenge. The petiolares group, consisting of about 30 species, grows well in a natural, acid, deciduous woodland in a cool aspect with pockets of accumulated leaf mould. One of the finest is *P. whitei* from Tibet and Bhutan. With variable china-blue to purple-hued blooms, it flowers early in spring. Regular division in damp spells

OPPOSITE: ORIGINALLY FROM YUNNAN IN SOUTHWEST CHINA, *PRIMULA SIKKIMENSIS*
PRODUCES RICHLY FRAGRANT YELLOW FLOWERS ON TALL, STATELY STEMS.

during late summer seems to suit *P. whitei* well and reduce the potential for vine-weevil. An easier choice in this section would be the later flowering *P.* 'Redpoll', a fine clone collected by Ludlow and Sherriff in 1949. It forms congested discs of dark red buds in later autumn and produces reddish-purple, stemless flowers in mid-spring. Growing in the same woodland conditions and of a similar nature is *P. boothii*, more readily available in its clean white form, *P. boothii alba*, found in Nepal by Tony Schilling.

One of my favourite primulas is *P. reptans*, which originates from the western Himalayas and belongs to the minutissimae section. *Primula reptans* is one of the few stoloniferous species and will grow best in a shallow trough with a lime-free, humus-rich, gritty soil medium. Positioned in a cool spot, this little treasure will reward its grower with a sea of purplish-violet flowers in late spring and early summer. Another favourite is *P. rosea*, which grows best in damp conditions. Planted shrewdly along a water course with *Lysichiton americanus* and the delicate

P. denticulata, this species with its carmine-pink umbels held on 20–30cm (8–12in) stems rates very highly. Closely related is the dainty *P. clarkei*, best tucked in between rocks in a cool position or in a trough. Division of this species every two or three years will ensure length of life and an annual production of clear pink flowers in late spring and early summer.

Each year, as summer approaches and temperatures rise, the most irresistible of species makes its appearance – *P. reidii* var. *williamsii*, which was first found by Stainton, Sykes and Williams in Nepal. The short 10–15cm (4–6in) stems each carry an umbel of beautiful powder-blue flowers, their delicious fragrance accentuated in early evening to attract night-flying moths to trigger the reproductive process. Good drainage and protection from the heat of the summer ensure success; saving seed provides the means for propagating this reliable perennial.

From Yunnan in southwest China come two lovely species – *P. sikkimensis* and *P. secundiflora* – the former with

ABOVE LEFT: *P. MARGINATA 'LINDA POPE'.* **ABOVE RIGHT:** *P. SECUNDIFLORA,* **A PLANT FROM CHINA THAT GROWS BEST IN A BOG GARDEN.**
OPPOSITE: THE STRIKING PINK CANDELBRA, *P. PULVERULENTA,* **ONE OF JIM JERMYN'S FAVOURITES; PLANT IT IN DRIFTS FOR BEST EFFECT.**

taller, stately stems carrying nodding umbels of richly fragrant yellow bells, the latter similarly scented with bold purple-red flowers. These primulas grow best in bog gardens or alongside streams.

Taking centre stage in these damp conditions are the candelabra primulas, many of which are the easiest primulas to grow in lime-free soil. They are typified by multi-tiered flower stems, often in excess of six tiers on stems 60–90cm (2–3ft) tall and offer considerable choice. Where natural light is abundant I would choose the following species and plant in generous drifts: *P. pulverulenta*, with reddish-purple flowers, would appear next to the striking orange-yellow *P. chungensis* and the clear yellow evergreen *P. helodoxa*. These species hybridise easily in the garden, producing attractive, pastel-shaded plants. Another candelabra worth mentioning is *P. japonica* from Japan, which usually has reddish-purple blooms and grows best in dappled shade rather than full light. This is available in several cultivars, the best being 'Miller's Crimson', a good dark red form, and 'Postford White', a vigorous large-flowered, white plant with an orange eye.

While the Himalayas are home to the lion's share of the 400 or so species of primula, the European Alps play host to a section of great importance horticulturally and historically – the auriculas. There is not space enough here to discuss the vast array of auriculas, yet mention must be made of a few of the more unusual species essential to the alpine collection, whether planted in troughs, dry walls, raised beds or in a rock garden.

Occupying the limestone crevices and cliffs in the Maritime Alps of southern France are two species with differing needs. *Primula allionii* flowering in early spring on south-facing-cliffs is a sight to behold, but recreating such a sight in your own garden is quite a different matter and can be a real challenge. Try a boulder of tufa rock, create a crevice with an overhang and plant vertically, then enjoy the reward of tight cushions of sticky foliage studded with bright pink flowers in early spring. By contrast, its neighbour *P. marginata* presents little in the way of a challenge, enjoying a freely drained chalky soil or being situated vertically in a cool position on a dry wall where its truncated, woody stems are hidden by clear, blue flowers with a pleasing fragrance in mid-spring. The form 'Linda Pope', possibly of hybrid origin, has a profusion of lilac flowers, epitomising the potential of this diverse race of the plants.

A final recommendation is *P. elatior*, one of the most reliable garden primulas, which is happy on either lime-free or chalky soils. This is the true oxlip and one of the parents of the tremendously popular polyanthus group. Growing up to 30cm (1ft), it bears up to 12 pale yellow flowers in a one-sided, drooping umbel. The finest form I have grown is the Turkish variant introduced by Jim and Jenny Archibald – *P. elatior* subsp. *pallasii*. This has strong stems that carry amazing umbels, top-heavy with huge, pale yellow flowers, which emit a sumptuous fragrance.

Primula is a genus most fittingly named by Linnaeus, providing some of the first flowers in our garden each spring and offering a number of prime garden plants for a variety of situations.

ABOVE: THE MAUVE-PINK POMPOMS OF *P. DENTICULATA.*

ABOVE: *P. ALLIONII* 'CLAUDE FLIGHT'.

ABOVE: *P. HELODOXA,* **A BEAUTIFUL EVERGREEN CANDELBRA PRIMULA.**
OPPOSITE: A CLOSE LOOK AT THE STUNNING *P. WHITEI.*

PROPAGATION

On the whole, all primulas can be comfortably propagated either by seed or division. Only a few species, mainly from the petiolares group, require seed to be sown immediately after collection. Sow seeds of hardy species on to a mixture of John Innes seed compost (preferably of a neutral to acid nature) and place containers in open frames. Seed is best sown in winter or early spring under glass. In summer, it is important that the seed frame is shaded from direct sunlight and that the pots are never allowed to dry out. Division should take place while the plant is in active growth and preferably during a damp spell. For many of the more vigorous species, it is necessary to divide congested clumps every two or three years for optimum performance.

CULTIVATION

Specific cultivation instructions are described above. However, there are a few general rules to observe. Nearly all primulas dislike extremes of temperature. Provide a cool position for some of the Himalayan species, since most merit shielding from the fiercest summer heat and need protection from the excesses of winter wetness. The use of cloches for winter protection and shading in summer should allow the more difficult species to be grown. In general, most primulas need a good water supply at the root and ample oxygen in the soil. This can be provided by organic material such as leaf-mould. It is advisable to move plants to fresh soil after five to seven years.

PESTS AND DISEASES

Problems arise in any concentrated collection of plants, but the blight of vine-weevil is particularly threatening to the primula grower and I write from experience of the dangers of growing them in smaller pots. If chemicals are to be avoided, and this must be a primary choice, frequent handling and division where appropriate, along with the regular removal of freshly fallen leaves and old growth, should provide a measure of protection. Biological control is only to be recommended under glass, where soil temperatures can be maintained at the specified level. To a lesser extent, primulas also suffer from viruses and botrytis. Viruses particularly seem to affect older stocks that have been regularly divided. Every five years it is beneficial to replenish old stock from seed origin.

Corydalis

orydalis is a large genus of around 450 species from the northern hemisphere. It includes tuberous dwarfs, climbing annuals, large herbaceous perennials and rock plants, recognisable by their ferny leaves and spikes of small, tubular flowers with snapdragon-like faces and long spurs. Colours range from palest cream to red, orange, yellow and brilliant blue. Around 60 species and 20 cultivars are listed in the *RHS Plant Finder*, and many are easy garden plants.

The easiest corydalis to grow in temperate climates are all woodland plants originating from Europe or eastern Asia. The European species are first to flower and often emerge with the snowdrops in early spring. My favourite is *Corydalis malkensis*, formerly *C. caucasica* var. *alba*, a tuberous perennial from the Caucasus. The stems uncurl a few inches from the ground, and have around eight pale green buds, which open into surprisingly large, pure white flowers with a wide, flat lip. Such a small, early-flowering plant is at the mercy of the weather, however, and can be best enjoyed grown in a pot, brought indoors while in flower but otherwise kept in a cool, shady place outside. This species was described in 1975 and its name comes from the Malka river, one of those torrents that flows down from the Caucasus mountains.

Almost as early flowering as *C. malkensis* is the most common of the tuberous species, *C. solida*. This is wild throughout mainland Europe from France to Russia and has been grown in British gardens for several centuries. In a few places in England and southern Scotland it has become naturalised, and some old books even record it as native in Britain. *Corydalis solida* is usually a rather dull reddish-purple but it can also be white, a bright red, a lovely, pure pink, a dark plum or nearly blue.

The red forms of *C. solida* are the most sought after, and the best known is now called *C. solida* subsp. *solida* 'George Baker', formerly called forma *transsylvanica*, which

OPPOSITE: 'NETTLETON PINK', **A CULTIVAR OF** *CORYDALIS SOLIDA* SUBSP. *SOLIDA* 'GEORGE BAKER'.

but soon makes a dense clump of tubers, which can be divided when dormant. Several other good clones have been named, including 'Nettleton Pink' and another pink, 'Beth Evans', which I have found slower to increase. A new one to look out for is the pale 'Blue Pearl', originating from Russia and Macedonia.

Later flowering than *C. solida* but also an excellent garden plant, is *C. cava*, which flowers in late spring. This is a more robust plant with stems up to 25cm (10in) tall, and a longer spike of usually pinkish flowers. It is distinguished from *C. solida* by the lack of a scale leaf near the base of the stem. The form I grow has white flowers and breeds true from seed. It came from the late Sir Cedric Morris, a painter and great gardener, who grew many rare bulbs in the walled garden of his house at Benton End in Suffolk, and here it grew in masses under old apple trees. *C. cava* has long been cultivated for its medicinal properties, and was found in most medieval herb gardens.

The aforementioned tuberous species from Europe are easy to grow. More difficult are those from the mountains of the Middle East and central Asia around Samarkand, Tashkent and Bishkek, where they are common in stony screes and under thorny bushes. *Corydalis ledebouriana* is a tuberous perennial from Uzbekistan, and has large flowers, usually with upward-pointing pale spurs and deep reddish lips. *Corydalis maracandica*, from near Samarkand, has a very thick spur, and often yellowish flowers. *Corydalis macrocentra* is one of the most showy, forming large clumps of bluish leaves and spikes of flowers that open yellow and fade to orange. I saw it growing on dry, sandy screes, which gives a clue to the cultivation of this whole group. They need to be kept moist in winter, and quite dry in summer – ideally in an alpine house, or in a large, deep pot in the greenhouse.

Until recently, bright blue corydalis were rare in cultivation, difficult to grow and expensive to buy. *Corydalis cashmeriana* was, and still is, the most beautiful – a miniature with intense, bright blue flowers. Unfortunately

originated in Romania. In my youth this was a plant of almost legendary rarity, grown by Ingwersen's, almost impossible to obtain and very slow to increase, but suddenly it seemed to increase more easily and became better known. Was a new introduction the cause of this sudden change? It has been suggested that a new introduction from the Transylvanian Alps in 1972 proved an easier grower, and it was from this that 'George Baker' was selected. The name was coined in 1977 to commemorate the great bulb grower from Sevenoaks.

Whatever its origin, 'George Baker' is a good plant for the open garden in deciduous shade and it grows well in a hot bulb frame, too. The stems are around 15cm (6in) tall, and about half this length is taken up by a crowded spike of up to 20 bright red flowers. It does not set seed by itself

ABOVE: *C. SOLIDA* SUBSP. *SOLIDA* 'GEORGE BAKER' **IS THE BEST KNOWN OF THE RED FORMS.**
OPPOSITE: **THE EVERGREEN, CLUMP-FORMING** *C. OCHROLEUCA* **MAKES THE PERFECT PARTNER FOR FERNS.**

it is not easy and being a high alpine from the Himalayas, only thrives in mountainous conditions such as in Scotland, where it is best in cool, sandy, peaty soil, among dwarf rhododendrons.

Nowadays, however, blue corydalis are the most common types, thanks to the ease of propagation of the Chinese herbaceous species *C. flexuosa*, a scaly-rooted, herbaceous plant that produces dense clusters of brilliant blue flowers in late spring and early summer. In May 1989, during a trip to China, James Compton, John d'Arcy and I found masses of this growing on the steep wooded sides of the Wolong and Baoxing valleys in western Sichuan. The

dainty blue flowers were set off by the fronds of the shuttlecock fern, *Matteuccia struthiopteris* – an unforgettable sight, and a combination easily copied in the garden.

We brought back some tiny pieces of the fleshy runners that the plant produces, and from these, three clones have come into cultivation – distinguished by their leaves. *Corydalis flexuosa* 'Père David' has bluish-green leaves, often marked with blood red, and is named after the original discoverer of the plant. 'China Blue' has brownish leaves, which become green in warm weather. 'Purple Leaf' is slightly smaller than the other two, with attractive dark purple leaves and flowers often flushed with purple.

ABOVE LEFT: 'PURPLE LEAF', **A CULTIVAR OF** *C. FLEXUOSA*, **WITH INTERESTING PURPLE-STAINED LEAVES AND DAINTY MAUVE FLOWERS.**
ABOVE RIGHT: *C. MALKENSIS*, **FORMERLY** *C. CAUCASICA* VAR. *ALBA,* **A TUBEROUS PERENNIAL FROM THE CAUCASUS.**

Two other clones are also grown but do not have runners and so are slower to propagate. 'Blue Panda', the first to be cultivated, was introduced in 1986 in America. It has narrower leaf lobes and smaller flowers of an excellent colour. 'Balang Mist', introduced by Chris Grey-Wilson, has very lovely, pale flowers above metallic, greyish leaves.

In Britain, all *C. flexuosa* produce leaves in autumn, and grow slowly through the winter before flowering in spring and early summer, in cool seasons continuing till autumn. In high summer the plants usually go dormant and may disappear completely before re-emerging in the cooler days of autumn. They are very easy to grow – and are widely available.

Corydalis elata, also from China, is similar to *C. flexuosa*, but comes later into leaf and flower. It responds well to rich feeding, when it can easily reach 30cm (1ft) or more in height. Another Chinese species, *C. mucronata*, has purple flowers with long upward-pointing spurs, which fade to buff. It is a long-lived and easily grown perennial for a damp place, and has just appeared in cultivation in Britain.

Yellow is a common colour in corydalis. The most familiar are the bright yellow *C. lutea*, and the similar creamy-yellow *C. ochroleuca*. These are rock plants and are lovely in old walls or crevices in the shade. Though the individual plants are not long-lived, and do not take kindly to being moved, they seed themselves in a restrained way.

In another yellow-flowered species, *C. cheilanthifolia*, the remarkably fern-like leaves are set in a rosette; this 'fern' then surprises us by putting up yellow flowers in later spring. It is a pretty but modest plant, and like *C. lutea* (yellow fumitory) it will seed itself in old walls and between rocks. It was introduced from China by E H Wilson around 1920.

A more robust species, of similar habit, is *C. nobilis* from Siberia, Mongolia and Chinese Turkestan, where we saw it

covering the sandy floor of a mountain valley. Considering it was introduced as long ago as 1783, it is rare in gardens in England, though it has become naturalised in Sweden. It has a fleshy tap root, and the stems reach about 50cm (20in) tall; the bright yellow flowers with a black throat are carried in short, dense spikes in spring. Judging by its habitat, the plant should be tolerant of summer drought and light shade, and therefore easy to grow in general garden conditions. It is, however, seldom seen for sale, unlike the forms of *C. flexuosa*, which are now common in garden centres, and the forms of *C. solida*, which can be obtained from most specialist garden nurseries.

ABOVE: THE BRILLIANT BLUE *C. FLEXUOSA,* A POPULAR CHINESE HERBACEOUS SPECIES.

ABOVE: A GOOD PLANT FOR THE ROCK GARDEN, THE YELLOW *C. CHEILANTHIFOLIA* IS RECOGNISED BY ITS DISTINCTIVE FERN-LIKE LEAVES.
OPPOSITE: *C. FLEXUOSA* 'CHINA BLUE'.

PROPAGATION

Tuberous species that have formed more than one growing point can be separated while dormant in summer, and replanted in autumn, but most are best grown from seed. Seed should be sown as fresh as possible in sandy, leafy compost. Most tuberous species make a single leaf in the first year, and this should be kept growing as long as possible so that a large enough tuber is formed to survive the summer. The herbaceous species seed freely, and young plants can be grown through the summer to flower the following year. Once they have made more than one crown they can be divided, which is best done in autumn.

CULTIVATION OF HERBACEOUS SPECIES

The herbaceous species are generally the easiest to grow. *Corydalis flexuosa* is widely available. Some people find it short-lived in the open garden, but it is easily cultivated once its needs are understood. It likes loose, fertile, leafy or peaty soil with lime, and will not grow in clay or acid conditions. The soil should be so loose that the whole plant can be easily scooped up. Divide and replant at least every other year in early autumn as soon as the leaves begin to appear; if not replanting, top-dress with leaf-mould or peat and sand with a general fertiliser and chalk or limestone added.

CULTIVATION OF TUBEROUS SPECIES

The European tuberous species such as *C. solida* and *C. cava* are easily grown in the open garden. They lie dormant in summer, when they should be cool and kept on the dry side. They need stony but leafy soil. The tuberous species from central Asia are better grown in a frame so they can be dried off in summer; they should be watered sparingly in winter. Most of their growing is done in spring. Keep them dry until mid- or late autumn, and then water carefully until spring. Late initial watering produces more compact and healthier plants. Compost should be sandy and very well drained.

SUN SEEKERS

Lilies

Of all bulbous plants, lilies are the most charismatic. Statuesque and elegant, they are valuable among perennials and shrubs in a border and can be grown equally well in containers. This profile of the genus focuses on the turk's-cap varieties that look so pleasing in a summer border.

I sincerely hope that I am never in the position to heed the Chinese assertion that, 'When you have only two pennies left in the world, buy a loaf of bread with one and a lily with the other'. In these dire circumstances, however, such action might have a certain appeal. After all, this combination would provide both sustenance and pleasure, as well as medicine if the going got even tougher, for there are many recommendations about the efficacy of lilies in treating maladies. Dioscorides extolled the value of a face pack of mashed madonna lily bulbs with honey, for it 'cleareth ye faces and makes them without wrinkles', and the leaves were reputedly an antidote to snake bites.

Epilepsy, internal parasites, lung infections and tumours were all cases for lily treatment but most of these involved *Lilium candidum*. Other species probably have similar properties and, in the 16th century, such an assumption led John Gerard to remark that God would not have created anything as beautiful as *L. martagon* to be without a use; it was just that he had not found out what that use was. Beautiful as they are, it seems that lilies also provided both medicine and food for thought.

Nevertheless, the aesthetic value of lilies was appreciated very early on and by the time of John Gerard, *L. bulbiferum*, *L. chalcedonicum*, *L. martagon* and the madonna lily, *L. candidum*, were well-known in English gardens. I cannot say that the first of these is my favourite lily. The gaudy, upward-facing cups of the orange lily *L. bulbiferum* are rather inelegant compared with the charm of the pendent turk's-cap types, and are without the grace of the heavily fragrant trumpet lilies. Reservations notwithstanding,

PREVIOUS PAGE: *SEDUM 'RUBY GLOW'*.
OPPOSITE: *LILIUM NEPALENSE,* **NATIVE TO NEPAL, GROWS TO ABOUT 1M (40IN) AND FLOWERS IN EARLY OR MIDSUMMER.**

L. bulbiferum is a good, robust garden plant and has been used by plant breeders to produce – through hybridisation – the vigorous group known as *L.* × *hollandicum*. Subsequently in the 1950s, largely through the inspired work of Jan de Haaff and his staff in Oregon, USA, the famous mid-century hybrids came on to the scene and 50 years on, we are still benefiting from these liaisons. One of the earliest of these, the orange, black-spotted hybrid 'Enchantment', is still popular, although it is now in competition with a great array of different coloured cultivars from white to pink, red, yellow and bicoloured.

Lilies belong to their own large family, *Liliaceae*, which includes tulips, fritillarias and erythroniums (dog's tooth violets), and they come in a range of colours and form to suit almost every taste and purpose. Although, due to the skill of the plant breeder, lily hybrids can now be counted in thousands, there are only about 100 wild species, distributed through the temperate regions of the northern hemisphere in Europe, Asia and North America.

These may for convenience be classified roughly on the overall form of their flowers. There are the familiar trumpet-shaped types like *L. regale*; those with bowl-shaped or saucer-like flowers held in an upward-facing position; and the charming turk's-cap lilies, whose flowers hang down with their petals curled elegantly backwards. The heavily fragrant oriental lilies, encompassing *L. auratum*, *L. speciosum* and their hybrids are also a recognised group.

Given the choice of only one kind of lily, I would have to choose the turk's-cap shape, such is its elegance, resulting from the sharply reflexed petals. Of the many species with this flower form, I find the red martagon of Constantinople, *L. chalcedonicum*, one of the most appealing – but also tantalising. Being a Mediterranean plant it does not conform to the usual growing conditions of the Asiatic lilies that mostly prefer a cool root run, whereas this scarlet turk's-cap is more at home in a warm, well drained alkaline soil – the antithesis of the cold, damp clay in my present

ABOVE LEFT: *L. LANCIFOLIUM,* **THE TIGER LILY. ABOVE RIGHT:** *L. PARDALINUM* **PRODUCES STRIKING RACEMES OF SPOTTED FLOWERS IN MIDSUMMER. OPPOSITE:** *L. HENRYI,* **GOOD IN PARTIAL SHADE.**

garden. The same sunny position will also suit another sealing-wax red lily from the Alpes Maritimes, *L. pomponium*, which is a worthy rival for its more easterly counterpart. However, ease of cultivation is a necessary consideration and, if one wishes for a red turk's-cap, the most certain investment would be a few bulbs of *L. pumilum*, a similar-looking lily from China and Tibet. Although not naturally long-lived, this is easy enough to grow, requiring only a well drained position, and it is one of the daintiest of all lilies with wiry stems clothed in numerous slender leaves. There is also a selection with yellow flowers known as 'Golden Gleam'. Having moved into the realm of the yellow turk's-caps, one must consider planting *L. pyrenaicum* since it is one of the few species that can be naturalised in grass. It is indeed happy in a range of situations, preferably far enough from the path for one to avoid its aroma, which is certainly not pleasant. Much

more impressive is its large relative from the Caucasus, *L. monadelphum* (also known as *L. szovitsianum*), which is also worth trying, especially in a patch of unkempt grass.

The early explorers in North America soon became aware of the native turk's-cap lilies growing there and these caused considerable interest when introduced into Europe. Two of the first to be introduced were *L. canadense*, in the early 17th century, and then *L. superbum*. The former is a most elegant plant, the yellow or red flowers bell-shaped with only slightly reflexed tips. But in the flamboyant orange-red *L. superbum*, and in its Californian relative *L. pardalinum*, they roll right back, revealing gaudily spotted interiors. The Asiatic species were largely unknown until the 19th and early 20th centuries when many were discovered, named and introduced. The now-familiar orange tiger lily (*L. lancifolium*), although cultivated for food by the Chinese over 1,000 years ago, did not arrive in

ABOVE LEFT: *L. CHALCEDONICUM*, **ONE OF THE MOST APPEALING TURK'S-CAPS, BUT NOT THE EASIEST TO GROW IN TEMPERATE CLIMATES.**
ABOVE RIGHT: *L. MONADELPHUM*, **ALSO KNOWN AS** *L. SZOVITSIANUM.*

the west until 1804. Undoubtedly this caused a stir among gardeners but nothing compared with the fuss that was made when *L. speciosum* appeared, introduced from Japan some 26 years later. This, in turn, was eclipsed by the arrival of *L. auratum*, the golden-rayed lily of Japan, which was an instant success. Only two years after its introduction, in 1864, it was reported that 'a large quantity' of bulbs were being auctioned at Covent Garden. After a journey of several months in a sailing vessel, 'most of them were as plump and fresh as if they had been dug up and brought from some suburban nursery on the morning of the sale'. *Lilium speciosum* and *L. auratum*, although still cultivated in their wild forms to a certain extent, are now somewhat overshadowed by the impressive range of oriental hybrids, heavily fragrant late-flowering cultivars, such as pure white 'Casa Blanca', crimson-banded 'Journey's End' and deep wine 'Black Beauty', a cross with the orange Chinese *L. henryi*.

The mention of lilies to many people will conjure up images of scented white trumpets in floral bouquets – usually *L. longiflorum*, the florist's favourite – and indeed there are many species like this, but now in a range of colours thanks to the skill of the plant breeder. However, among all the highly bred descendants of the wild forms, *L. regale*, the regal lily must remain one of the most charismatic. Introduced in the early part of the 20th century by Ernest Wilson, it was not long before the cultivated stock of *L. regale* was reputed to be 250,000 bulbs, selling at a price of £20 per 1,000, an indication of the ease of its cultivation. Of the wild species of trumpet lily *L. regale* is clearly the best garden plant among them, but the hybrid trumpets of today are also easily pleased and come in a wide range of colours unknown in nature: from the rich pinkish-purple of Pink Perfection Group to deep orange-apricot in African Queen Group and the chartreuse-flushed 'Green Magic'.

ABOVE: THE BEAUTIFUL *L. MARTAGON,* THE COMMON TURK'S-CAP, IS A VIGOROUS, CLUMP-FORMING SPECIES, WHICH WILL GROW HAPPILY IN LEAFY SOIL WHETHER POSITIONED IN FULL SUN OR PARTIAL SHADE.

ABOVE: *L. PYRENAICUM,* WHICH IS IDEAL FOR NATURALISING IN GRASS.

PROPAGATION

Lilies can be grown from seed quite easily, and this is a very satisfactory method of acquiring fresh, virus-free young plants – although it will take up to seven years for them to flower (some of the hybrids will flower after just two years, while species such as *Lilium martagon* take longer). It is quicker to try raising some by breaking a few scales off the parent bulbs. This can be done at almost any time, but midsummer or autumn is best. If the bulb is still growing, scrape away the soil until the bulb can be seen and then snap off a few of its outer scales; this will do no harm. Wash the scales in a fungicide solution and place them in a polythene bag of slightly damp Perlite, Vermiculite or clean, sharp sand in a warm room at about 20°C (68°F). It takes three to five weeks for small bulbs to form on the broken surfaces and, as soon as roots appear, these can be detached and potted up or planted out. They take one to two years to produce flowering plants.

CULTIVATION

Most lilies do well in a site where their bulbs will be shaded by low-growing shrubs or perennials with their stems poking through into the sunlight, or in the dappled shade of taller trees and shrubs. A few of the sun-lovers, such as *L. candidum* and *L. chalcedonicum*, need a more open, warmer situation, like a south wall. Before planting, dig a liberal amount of well rotted organic matter (not peat or fresh manure), work in a little balanced fertiliser and add some sharp sand if the drainage is poor. The larger lilies need about 40cm (16in) between bulbs and to be 15–20cm (6–8in) deep, but smaller varieties can go in at about 10–15cm (4–6in) apart and equally deep. *Lilium candidum* is an exception: the bulbs are planted with their tips just below soil level. Most lilies can be grown on alkaline soils, providing there is a good humus content. The oriental species *L. speciosum* and *L auratum*, however, require lime-free conditions.

PESTS AND DISEASES

Lily-growers in southern Britain and Europe need to keep a sharp eye open in spring when the lilies emerge, as they – and the related fritillaries – attract a bright red beetle that has a ravenous appetite for lily foliage. Lily beetles, as they are known, should be ruthlessly hunted down and destroyed before they have a chance to lay their eggs on the underside of the leaves. Allowed to develop into larvae that are equally ravenous and cover themselves with a jacket of their own excrement, they will completely defoliate a plant with ease. Frequent hand-picking is the best remedy, although any insecticide will also do the trick. Catching them requires some practice for, at the slightest hint of danger, they drop to the ground and feign death, usually upside-down with their black underparts uppermost so they are difficult to see. It is also important to control aphids since, apart from causing distorted shoots, they can transmit viral diseases, for which there is no remedy. The signs of a virus are distorted leaves and flowers, and the only course is to destroy infected plants and raise new stock from seed, or buy bulbs that are guaranteed virus-free. Botrytis, which usually manifests itself as dark blotches on the foliage, should be controlled with regular applications of fungicide during the growing season. Use any approved brand recommended for the treatment of botrytis.

LILIES IN CONTAINERS

If lilies do not thrive in your garden, try them in earthenware or wooden containers, which are generally very satisfactory. One bulb of a large lily needs a 22cm (9in) diameter pot, whereas the same pot would take three to five bulbs of the smaller types. Use an open, well drained soil such as a one part loam, one part leaf mould and one part sharp sand mixture, enriched with a general balanced fertiliser. The bulbs are placed about two thirds of the way down the pot and covered, leaving 5cm (2in) between the soil surface and the rim so that more compost can be added in summer. Keep the containers in a cool place for the winter, preferably raising them off the ground to help drainage. As they begin to shoot in spring, give them more water and light, moving them to their final positions for flowering. When the lilies die down in autumn the stems should be cut off and the bulbs either re-potted, if they are in small containers, or top-dressed if in large ones. As long as they remain healthy and not too congested they can remain for three years or more in the same pots.

Phormiums

No other evergreen perennials offer such a spectrum of colour as New Zealand flax, or phormiums, from the standard grey-green flax of *Phormium tenax* through to golds, creams, pinks, purple and even black. This kaleidoscope of colour is reflected in the bizarre collection of names that phormium cultivars come under, from 'Bronze Baby', 'Dazzler' and 'Sundowner', to 'Copper Beauty' and 'Apricot Queen'.

Phormiums are widely grown in gardens all around the world, but it is only relatively recently that they have been cultivated as ornamental plants. Long before phormiums were first described, by a botanist on Captain Cook's second voyage to New Zealand in 1776, the plants had been used by the Maoris, their fibrous leaves woven into clothing, matting and containers – hence the name, which derives from the Greek *phormion* meaning mat. The Maoris also used flax gum and roots as an antiseptic. Many of the numerous cultivars available today are thanks to the New Zealand hybridiser Margaret Jones, who spotted an unusual sport from *P. cookianum* subsp. *hookeri* 'Tricolor' 30 years ago. In 1978 this was marketed as 'Cream Delight', the first of many cultivars now widely available all over the world.

Phormiums come in a variety of sizes, including several dwarf cultivars. There are two species in the genus: *P. tenax* (also known as coastal flax, or *harakeke* by the Maoris), which can reach 3m (10ft) in height with upright leaves, and *P. cookianum* (mountain flax or *wharakiki*), which grows up to 2m (6½ft) but with a more lax habit than *P. tenax*. Both will spread to at least 1m (40in) in width. In New Zealand, *P. tenax* flourishes near water, whereas the smaller *P. cookianum* grows on hillsides. A more elegant plant, *P. cookianum* has graceful arching leaves that move in the breeze. Phormiums are hardier than many people think, surviving temperatures down to -12°C (10°F), but I would make sure they are planted in well drained soil to prevent

OPPOSITE: THE EXUBERANT SWORD-LIKE FOLIAGE OF *PHORMIUM* 'JESTER'.

soggy roots from freezing in winter.

If you wish to create impact, then look no further than *P. tenax*, which appears to erupt out of the earth and grows to well over 2m (6½ft). 'Goliath' is the most impressive and is a must if you are into bold foliage. It has grey-green leaves, which soar to 3m (10ft) in height, and flower spikes that can top this by up to 1m (40in). If grey-green foliage doesn't shout enough for you, then opt for a striking bronze or purple form. 'Bronze Baby' is a good dwarf plant with red-tinted foliage reaching only 1m (40in), and is therefore manageable in most gardens. If choosing from the widely available Purpureum Group, choose the darkest specimens you can find, deep purple-blacks, as some can verge on muddy-brown. Another excellent cultivar is 'Sundowner', which grows to 2m (6½ft) and is a blend of bronze-green with rose-pink margins. Good dark cultivars include 'Tom Thumb', which is less than 1m (40in) tall with bright-green leaves and red-bronze margins, and 'Platt's Black', which as the name suggests has very dark leaves.

Of the cookianum varieties I have found *P. cookianum* subsp. *hookeri* 'Tricolor' to be the most vigorous and hardy. It has cream and green leaves with a red margin – enough to make any border sizzle. The reverse of the leaf is just as interesting, like an exotic bar code. The leaves are wind-resistant and do not demonstrate signs of ageing. Its progeny 'Cream Delight' will illuminate your garden with its light, creamy leaves. It is also hardy, though not quite as vigorous as the parent plant. Another brightly coloured cultivar is 'Yellow Wave', which you should avoid if you have a horror of gold foliage. However I find its presence unusually cheerful as I live in an area where we get more than our fair share of wet or overcast days. The only downside is this plant's tendency to form rust on the leaves. It is apparently caused by the damp climate and is something you have to live with – or remove the affected leaves. Mature 'Tricolor' plants may reach approximately 1.5m (5ft), but they take almost a decade to grow to this height. There are some huge specimens at Mount Stewart gardens in Ireland.

ABOVE LEFT: CONTRASTING RED AND GREEN STRIPES ON *P.* 'SUNDOWNER'. ABOVE RIGHT: LIME GREEN AND CREAM *P.* 'RADIANCE'.
OPPOSITE: USE *P. COOKIANUM* SUBSP. *HOOKERI* 'CREAM DELIGHT' TO BRIGHTEN UP GLOOMY CORNERS.

Phormiums throw out Jack-and-the-beanstalk-like flower stems in summer, which in time develop into seed pods. *Phormium tenax* has orange-red flowers that can reach up to 4m (13ft) on an established plant, while *P. cookianum* cultivars have greenish-yellow flowers. Once the tantalising strelitzia-like buds have opened, the flowers are unremarkable and tiny in relation to the stem, but they are rich in nectar, which attracts pollinating birds in the wild. Reminiscent of runner beans, the long-lasting, nut-brown seed-pods make up for the lack of impact from the flowers. They grow upwards on *P. tenax*, whereas they are more twisted in *P. cookianum* and dangle down from the stem. Although many people will want to remove the stems in the autumn, I leave them to add height throughout winter.

Once you have introduced one of these bold plants into your garden you may wonder what other plants to plant with it. Such extrovert foliage calls for something with equal weight or a complete contrast. The sword-like leaves are made even more distinct when thrusting up between the leathery foliage of *Fatsia japonica*, while tender *Ricinus communis* makes an equally efficient foil in summer. Virtually anything exotic makes a good companion to phormiums and it makes sense to use other plants from New Zealand. For a different shape and form look no further than corokias with their tiny platinum leaves and contorted stems, especially *Corokia cotoneaster*, which is so twisted that it looks like something that might grow on the moon. Pittosporums also work well – their small leaves and variety of leaf colour can be used to echo that of the phormiums.

The colourful personalities and architectural merits of these plants are mesmerising. In summer, phormiums lend an exotic touch and they more than pay their way in winter. In the garden, it is impossible to go wrong with strong shapes and good foliage colour, so what are you waiting for?

ABOVE: *P. TENAX* 'DAZZLER' **PRODUCES FOLIAGE IN STRIKING, FIERY HUES.**
OPPOSITE: **BLOOD RED BLOOMS ON ARCHITECTURAL STEMS OF** *P. TENAX* PURPUREUM GROUP.

ABOVE: **SURPRISINGLY** *P. COOKIANUM* SUBSP. *HOOKERI* 'TRICOLOR' **WILL COPE WITH TEMPERATURES WELL BELOW FREEZING.**

OPPOSITE: AN INTRICATELY CONSTRUCTED FLOWER OF *P. TENAX.*

CULTIVATION

Phormiums are ideal if you live by the sea and enjoy mild winters. They should, however, withstand temperatures down to -12°C (10°F) and probably more, depending on their location, age and variety. They dislike freezing wind as it shreds the leaves, and they will not withstand heavy frosts, particularly when pot-grown, so they appreciate the shelter of sunny walls. The pink-striped cultivars are slightly less hardy, so position them sensibly. Phormiums do not do well on heavy clay soil that is water-logged in winter – they must have the best of both worlds and thrive in moist but well drained soil. From my own experience, I have found that they prefer being planted in compost and benefit from watering rather than feeding. However, without feeding the colours may fade or revert, and in this case a liquid feed would be beneficial. Alternatively, when a shoot of an unwanted colour emerges on a hybrid plant, it should be cut off at the base. Removal of older leaves in spring will encourage more showy juvenile foliage. Water heavily in the first growing season and mulch before winter. Once settled, the plant will withstand drought and only require the minimum of maintenance. Phormiums grow fast in pots so remember to re-pot every couple of years. When planted in the soil it is vital to make sure you have chosen the right position. Phormiums are focal-point plants and should be sited accordingly. Bear in mind their eventual height and spread when planting near windows or near a path – their typical spread will be will over 1m (40in). It is difficult to move phormiums because they will lose their leaves in shock but, if re-sited successfully, the plant should recover after a few seasons. It is better to cut the leaves back by half when transplanting a mature plant.

PROPAGATION

Sow seed at 13–18°C (55–64°F) in spring. Divide in spring, but only try this with a mature specimen. Try and slice as deeply as possible to extricate the most root. Unfortunately the foliage far outweighs the amount of root, so cut the foliage back by half to help rejuvenate the plant and keep well watered. If you retain the foliage, prune any dying leaves as necessary. New leaves will soon grow from the centre.

PESTS AND DISEASES

Phormiums are, happily, very resistant to pests and diseases but mealy-bug can be a problem under glass or in warmer climates. Slugs and snails are prone to lurk in the core of the plant where it's cool and damp and may attack leaves from the inside out.

Lavender

Herbalists of the 16th and 17th centuries frequently referred to lavender as 'a hot and airy plant which is especially useful against cold diseases of the head'. It is curious that the so-called 'hot' nature of the plant allegedly cured cold ailments. Parkinson says 'the dried flowers dry up the moisture of a cold brain'. So typically English has lavender become that it is important to be reminded that the plant's real home lies in hotter climates.

Gerard, in his 1596 *Herball*, illustrates seven lavender plants, five of which are easily recognised as separate species. The best known is *Lavandula angustifolia*, narrow-leaved lavender, and three of Gerard's illustrations portray some variations of this species. It is usually called 'spike' because of the shape of the flower stems, but this name was also used for other species. The ancient Greeks called another lavender *nardus*, and it is possible that the 'spikenard' of the bible was in fact this plant. The word lavender itself derives from *lavare*, to wash, and indicates how the flowers were used for fragrance in Roman times. Lavender oil distilled in alcohol was always sold in the *officina* or apothecary's shop as *Oleum Spicae*.

As well as the oil, both leaves and flowers are powerfully fragrant. The flowers are dried and sewn into sachets for scenting linen and leather. They are also used in cooking for flavouring sugar, jam and even ice-cream. Lavender is a favourite ingredient in pot-pourri and shampoos and the oil is burnt at funerals and used for embalming in Mediterranean countries.

There are some 30 species of lavender in all. The greatest density is found in the western Mediterranean, with some occurring in the Canary Isles and Madeira. Others reach east to Turkey, East Africa, Arabia and even into southern India. All lavenders are xerophytes – that is, plants adapted to heat and drought, producing narrow, often hairy leaves, and the characteristic oils as a protection

OPPOSITE: PERFUMED CLOUDS OF THE FRENCH LAVENDER, *LAVANDULA STOECHAS.*

slopes of what is now south London were cultivated lavender fields – hence Lavender Hill in Battersea. Over the centuries many selected forms have been bred. In the 18th century, a white-flowered form, *L. angustifolia* 'Alba', was prized as a separate species – this form can still be found growing today. There is also a dwarf, white-flowered form known as *L. angustifolia* 'Nana Alba', which grows barely 30cm (1ft) tall. *Lavandula* 'Rosea' and the paler *L.* 'Loddon Pink' are two pink-flowered forms, both with eau-de-cologne-scented leaves.

It is still hard to match the free-flowering, deep, almost electric-blue 'Hidcote', with its short stature and purple calyces enclosing the flowers. 'Munstead' is similar but paler. *Lavandula latifolia* is a larger, broad-leaved lavender with much-branched flowering stems. It is a rather ungainly plant, with top-heavy stems and flowers, which are liable to flop.

This is the other parent of *L.* × *intermedia*, often called Dutch lavenders, including 'Hidcote Giant', which reaches 1.2m (4ft) tall. This deep blue cultivar should not be confused with 'Hidcote'. 'Seal', another tall plant, has much paler flowers. 'Grosso' is an excellent cultivar with large, purplish-blue spikes on a shorter stem.

Lavandula lanata is almost as hardy as *L.* × *intermedia* but suffers from rot on its wide, felted, silver-grey leaves. Originally from southern Spain, this plant is notable for the beauty of its leaves and not its rather insignificant flowers. Many plants sold as *L. lanata* are actually a hairy form of *L. latifolia*, which is greener. In winter, it is worth covering young *lanata* plants with panes of glass to keep the rain off.

French lavender, *L. stoechas*, is a variable species with three distinct subspecies, found around the Mediterranean from Spain to Turkey. It was called 'Sticadore' by early herbalists, derived from the Greek *stichos*, a row or line, which referred to the formation of the flowers in four angled ranks. So common was this plant on a group of

against dessication. They grow on exposed hillsides, usually among rocks, in hot, dry and often windswept places.

Lavandula angustifolia has also been known as *L. vera*, *L. officinalis* and *L. spica*, but many of these names have been found to refer to the hybrid *L.* × *intermedia*. *Lavandula angustifolia* is easily recognised by its straight, unbranched spikes and narrow leaves. It is the hardiest of the *Lavandula* species, capable of withstanding frosts of -15°C (5°F). It is often called English or common lavender because England once produced the finest lavender oil. A century ago, Mitcham in Surrey was the world centre for the production of this oil and the south-facing, well drained

ABOVE: THE CURIOUS BLOOMS OF *L. PINNATA* APPEAR ON LONG STEMS IN MIDSUMMER.
OPPOSITE: *L. STOECHAS* CAN BE IDENTIFIED BY ITS CONSPICUOUS BRACTS.

flower stems. Unfortunately this species group is not as frost-hardy as the others – frost and winter damp can wreak havoc unless they are planted in very sheltered positions.

Closely related is another beautiful lavender with dentate or toothed leaves, which often have curiously rolled margins. This is *L. dentata*. The bracts are sometimes absent from this species, although some beautiful lilac bracted forms are found on the Balearic Islands. *Lavandula dentata* has another form found in north Africa and the Canary Islands with silver-white leaves, called *L. d. candicans*. Many of these less hardy species make superb pot plants, grown in clay pots. Given the benefit of the extra warmth of a greenhouse early in the year, *L. dentata* can be flowering in Britain in early spring. Some Canary Island species, such as the glaucous-leaved *L. pinnata*, will flower in the middle of winter if the conditions are light, airy and reasonably warm. They thrive on a little watering in winter and plenty once growth begins in early spring. Pots can be brought outside in summer.

Some tender lavenders may appeal to the ardent lavenderphile, such as the tender *L. pinnata* or the aromatic curiosity, *L. viridis*, which, as its name implies, is almost entirely green with occasional narrow, green bracts above the flower stems – revealing its relationship to *L. stoechas*. It is found in Spain, Portugal and Madeira and has very strongly-scented, sticky, loose leaves and greenish-white flowers.

Lavandula multifida is also tender, with deeply-lobed, almost pinnate leaves and multi-branched stems, covered in hairs. It is very free-flowering and can be grown as an annual, flowering in late summer.

The last word on lavender should be left to Culpepper, the great herbalist, who says in his *Pharmacopoeia* of 1653, 'two spoonfulls of the distilled waters of the flowers taken, restores a lost voice and also the tremblings and passions of the heart'.

islands off the French coast that they became known as the Stoechades (now the Iles d'Hyères). Most flowering stems of this species possess showy plumes of colourful, enlarged bracts. The flowers themselves vary in colour from almost black to white or pink; the bracts vary in colour and size.

All forms of *L. stoechas* except subspecies *pedunculata* produce short, flowering stems, which barely rise out of the linear leaves. *Lavandula stoechas* subsp. *pedunculata* was once regarded as a separate species. This is a striking plant that grows in Spain and northern Portugal. In this form, the stems are carried high above the plant and possess deep pinkish-red bracts, which wave like banners above the

ABOVE: UNLIKE MOST OF ITS RELATIVES, *L. VIRIDIS* PRODUCES PALE GREEN SPIKES OF FLOWERS.

ABOVE: A FINE CLUMP OF *L. ANGUSTIFOLIA* 'ROSEA'.

ABOVE: *L. X INTERMEDIA* **MIXES WELL WITH THE LIME-GREEN FLOWERS OF LADY'S MANTLE,** *ALCHEMILLA MOLLIS.*
OPPOSITE LEFT: *L. ANGUSTIFOLIA* 'MUNSTEAD'. **OPPOSITE RIGHT:** *L. STOECHAS* SUBSP. *PEDUNCULATA.*

CULTIVATION

Lavender is often sold in containers growing in loamless, peaty compost, which can cause problems later. In cold winters lavender sitting in wet peat will simply rot and die. During dry summers, peat is notoriously difficult to re-wet and roots used to moisture will shrivel. If possible, buy bare-rooted plants in autumn or plants grown in loam with added grit.

Old plants look their best on sunny banks where the drainage is free, or tumbling over retaining walls, which reflect the heat, ripening the wood and intensifying the aroma of the oils. After 10–15 years, hardy lavenders become straggly and untidy. Youth and vigour can be prolonged by careful clipping in the spring and again in late summer.

PROPAGATION

Old plants can be used for new cuttings, which root very easily in summer. Once rooted, the old parent plant can be planted out in a sheltered spot and 'tried' for hardiness.

Propagate lavender from semi-ripe cuttings, 7–10cm (3–4in) long, taken in mid- to late summer from healthy-looking, non-flowering shoots. Remove the soft growth from the tip of the shoot and trim the leaves from the bottom half of the cutting. Dip the cuttings in hormone rooting powder and plant them in an outdoor nursery bed of loam-free potting compost, covering it with a large cloche or plastic tunnel. Alternatively, plant the cuttings in a cold frame, to a depth of 15–20cm (6–8in). Insulate the cold frame or cloche to protect from frost. Slowly harden off the rooted cuttings, which can then be planted out into their flowering positions in mid- to late spring.

Eucomis

Native to mountainous regions of South Africa, eucomis is an unusual bulbous plant grown for its waxy flowers and curious shapes, that should be better known by gardeners.

A good friend and gardener once said, 'A garden with a eucomis is a garden full of promise'. So it is strange that, 270 years after the first plant was grown in Britain, eucomis are rarely seen. Climate and tastes can change rapidly, yet perhaps their star is now rising along with the ever-increasing demand for the unusual. Their subtle flower colours, waxy texture and curious shapes certainly provoke comment. One imaginative observer thought that the prostrate stems, heavily pregnant with seedpods and appearing as if studded with rusty nails, were perfectly fashioned for use in the arena by gladiators.

Many people confuse eucomis with foxtail lilies (*Eremurus*), which they resemble, but eucomis are much easier to grow. Members of the family Hyacinthaceae, the first specimen from an English garden was described in 1732 by Dillenius, professor of botany at Oxford University. He did not use the name we know today but named the plant *corona regalis lilii folio crenato*, meaning the 'crown royal lily with crenate leaves'. Nearly 60 years later the French botanist, L'Heritier, named them eucomis from the Greek *eu*, meaning good, and *kome* meaning hair or tuft and referring to the crown of leafy bracts at the top of each flower spike. This has given them the common name of pineapple lily.

There are only ten species of eucomis and these are mostly from South Africa. All but one of these come from the summer rainfall areas often at high altitudes, up to 3,000 metres, where they flower from early to late summer. In more temperate northern climates they continue to flower from midsummer to early autumn but still demand a constant supply of water and as much sunshine as possible. The one winter rainfall species, *Eucomis regia*,

OPPOSITE: EXOTIC AND UNUSUAL, *EUCOMIS HUMILIS* PRODUCES RACEMES OF STAR-LIKE FLOWERS.

comes from the southwestern Cape of South Africa. Rare in cultivation, cool wet weather will trigger its growth but as this species is not hardy in the northern hemisphere it is best grown in a container under glass.

For general garden effect the most dramatic species is *E. comosa* in all its forms. This is a tall plant, up to 1m (40in) high, and the flower colours range from pale green through to cream, and pink to purple. An added bonus is the developing ovaries, which swell and glisten becoming suffused with red-wine tints like tiny candied beetroots. In some forms the flowers have a delicate coconut scent. Furthermore, some selections in cultivation now have the most amazing purple leaves, which are particularly noticeable in early summer, such as 'Zeal Bronze' from Terry Jones in Devon and 'Sparkling Burgundy' from New Zealand.

Eucomis bicolor is one of the most widely available species. Introduced in 1878 to the famous Veitch nursery in

ABOVE LEFT AND RIGHT: *E. COMOSA;* THE LEAFY BRACTS AT THE TOP OF EACH FLOWER SPIKE HAVE EARNED EUCOMIS THE COMMON NAME OF PINEAPPLE LILY. OPPOSITE: *E. PALLIDIFLORA* IS THE LARGEST OF THE SPECIES.

could only be achieved in really warm climates or under glass. *Eucomis pole-evansii* is another tall, stately species, but is, I believe, hardly different from *E. pallidiflora*.

Eucomis zambesiaca flowers in mid- or late summer in Britain and was so named to distinguish it from the earlier discovery of *E. regia*, a rare spring-flowering species in its native southwestern Cape. *Eucomis zambesiaca* is a much smaller plant than any of the above, being at most 30cm (1ft) in full bloom, with white flowers ageing to green. Being of dainty stature, it is ideal for growing in pots and has a sweet if faint scent of coconut.

The remaining species are rare in cultivation and are probably not garden-worthy in Britain, but in sunnier climes make interesting curiosities. Although I have never seen *E. humilis*, it grows successfully out of doors at the Royal Botanic Gardens, Kew, and sounds very tempting with its dark purple filaments and ovary. *Eucomis schijffii* was first described in 1976 and is the smallest of all the species, with strange metallic purple or brownish leaves and flowers the colour of vintage port. Collected at an altitude of 2,800 metres (9,180ft), it might prove to be tolerably hardy.

For those with good soil and enough sunshine, eucomis are worth trying. Plant with *Gladiolus papilio*, which matches the eucomis in height and complements the muted flower colours. In contrast, small grasses provide an airy foil against the denser forms of eucomis; they also enjoy similar conditions. For late colour associations, try hardy chrysanthemums, such as the crimson 'Emperor of China', or 'Mary Stoker', which is the colour of old straw. As they break into flower, they echo the fading colours of eucomis in early autumn. These plants are no more difficult to grow than *Nerine bowdenii* and give nearly three months of interest while adding an air of tropical exuberance. With so many plants from the Cape already established in British gardens, eucomis should at least be given a chance.

London, the wonderful jade-green flowers are thick and waxy in texture. They are unique to the genus, with their claret-edged flowers that complement the mottled undersides of the leaves. The only negative side to this easy-to-grow species is the rank smell of the flowers, reminiscent of cabbage water. The paler green form, *E. bicolor* 'Alba', which could be described as apple-white, does not have purple edges to the flowers although it does share the same personal hygiene problems.

Eucomis pallidiflora, the third of the large garden-worthy species, lacks the dark purple or brown tones evident in *E. comosa*. When grown well it is the largest species of all, growing to nearly 1.75m (5¾ft), although realistically this

ABOVE: DESPITE ITS FOETID SCENT, *E. BICOLOR* **IS GROWN FOR ITS THICKLY TEXTURED, WAVY FOLIAGE.**
OPPOSITE: **A NICELY COLOURED SELECTION OF** *E. COMOSA.*

ABOVE: THE WAXY BLOOMS OF *E. BICOLOR.* OPPOSITE: *E. COMOSA,* THE MOST DRAMATIC OF ALL THE SPECIES; UP TO 1M (40IN) TALL, IT
TAKES MANY FORMS WITH FLOWERS RANGING FROM PALE GREEN TO PURPLE.

CULTIVATION

Sunshine and moisture are the two key elements essential for success when growing eucomis. They cannot flourish or flower properly if they are denied either of these. In temperate climates, eucomis should be planted in a position that receives as much sunshine as possible, open but sheltered and ideally at the base of a south-facing wall. Having said that, we have no such walls at the nursery in Somerset, so they are grown in open nursery beds in full sun, lightly mulched in winter. Whether they are grown in the ground or large pots, they need their own space and do not want to be crowded by other plants. Well drained soil has often been quoted as a prerequisite but, if this is chalky or sandy, it could be too dry in the summer when the plants need all the water they can get. Certainly the larger-growing forms flower well and clump up on our rich heavy soil, which is often very soggy after prolonged rainfall.

Our gardening friends in warmer latitudes should have few problems in establishing and maintaining healthy colonies of eucomis – they are, after all, children of the sun. Bulbs grown in pots or tubs are obviously susceptible to freezing but, planted at least 15cm (6in) deep and with a slight mulch, those in the ground can be considered hardy in Britain, especially in sheltered gardens.

PROPAGATION

There are three easy ways for the gardener to increase stock. The first is natural division of established clumps either from the ground or large pots. This is best done in early spring before the new shoots are too advanced. Use a sharp knife to cut cleanly including some of the basal plate – trying to force the plant apart by hand can often leave this behind. Any large areas of wounding can be left to dry in the air for a few days before replanting; this helps prevent any rot appearing in case the bulbs get too wet.

The second method is by seed. Some of the larger species such as *Eucomis comosa* can have over 150 individual flowers each with their own ovaries producing up to 10 seeds. The reality is somewhat different, however, as early frosts can destroy the potential of ripening seed heads. Bulbs grown under glass or in pots will safely yield fully ripe seed; once collected in autumn as the seed cases split open, it need not be sown until spring warmth encourages germination. After the first year in a deep seed tray, the seedlings will need to be spaced out for a second growing season in pots or trays before they are large enough to plant out. This should be done in spring, just before full root growth commences. The seedlings will all be slightly different, particularly if several species and hybrids are grown in close proximity. With regular liquid feeding, they should flower in their third year but the largest species will probably need one more. Insects including butter-flies, wasps and green-bottle flies adore the nectar-rich flowers.

If you do have an outstanding form, which you want to propagate vegetatively and quickly, taking leaf cuttings is the third option. This involves cutting the leaf across its length into strips 2.5cm (1in) wide, dipping them in fungicide and pressing them vertically into a 50:50 mix of peat and Vermiculite so the strips are half buried. This should be done in early summer. Cover the leaf cuttings loosely with polythene to prevent desiccation, taking care that it does not come into immediate contact with them as condensation may cause damping off. It will appear as if nothing is happening for the first ten weeks but roots slowly form and, by the autumn, the polythene can be removed. As if by magic, tiny bulbs, like a string of pearls, will have formed below the dying leaf. These can be potted on the following spring.

Eremurus

From the harsh terrain and extreme climate of the Middle East and Central Asia, the genus *Eremurus* has become a familiar sight in temperate gardens. Eremurus are best known as foxtail lilies but their magnificent spires of colour have inspired several other vivid common names, including desert candle, king's spear and giant asphodel. The latter alludes to the loose relationship that eremurus has with the genus *Asphodelus*. Eremurus are left alone by grazing animals and occur in considerable quantities where other herbage has been overgrazed.

Classified in 1818 by Friedrich Marschall von Bieberstein, the name eremurus is derived from the Greek *eremos*, meaning desert and *oura*, meaning tail – referring to the tall spikes of flowers. These bulbous herbaceous perennials are natives of the open deserts, grassland and mountainsides of the Middle East, Central Asia and the foothills of the Himalayas, and as such are exposed to extremes of temperature and weather conditions throughout the season. During the winter, temperatures can plummet to -40°C (-40°F), and the dormant plant is covered in a blanket of snow. As the temperatures rise in the spring, the snow melts and new leaf growth is triggered. In the searing summer heat, the leaves die down before the plant flowers and, once flowering is over, it becomes dormant again and the crown is baked by the fierce desert sun. However, despite the extremes they encounter in their natural habitats, eremurus do very well as garden plants in Britain, Europe and North America. But, due to the high levels of rainfall in these regions, they will only tolerate temperature drops to a maximum of -5°C (23°F). As a consequence, they need protection from late spring frosts but thrive in well drained soil and full sun.

Eremurus produce a clump of strap-shaped leaves and majestic flower spikes that reach heights of up to 3m (10ft) tall, rising from a crown surrounded by a mass of fleshy roots, resembling an oversized starfish. Masses of tiny

OPPOSITE: AN EARLY-FLOWERING SPECIES, *EREMURUS HIMALAICUS* IS ONE OF THE EASIEST TO ESTABLISH IN THE GARDEN.

available than others. Several originate from Afghanistan such as *Eremurus aitchisonii*, which grows to 2m (6½ft) in height and has pink flowers – its white form, 'Albus' is occasionally available at nurseries. *Eremurus aitchisonii* flowers relatively early, in late spring, and there are several popular cultivars such as 'Emmy Ro', which has clear yellow flowers and 'Harmony' with shell-pink flowers.

Eremurus robustus was introduced in 1874 from eastern Turkey, Central Asia and Afghanistan – where it grows up to 3,500 metres (11,500ft) above sea level. It is one of the most magnificent species and makes a splendid garden plant. Given full sun and well drained soil it will produce towering spikes of up to 3m (10ft), smothered in pink flowers with a brown blotch at their base. They remain in bloom for several weeks during mid- and late summer, creating an extraordinary display.

Another of the early-flowering species, is *E. himalaicus*, which was introduced in 1881 and comes from Afghanistan and the western Himalayas. With an abundance of pure white flowers on a dense cylindrical spike, it reaches up to 2.5m (8ft); it is one of the species most easily obtained from nurseries and one of the easiest to establish in the garden. 'Image' is the only cultivar of this species available with soft-yellow flowers tinged with green on the outside.

In the same year, *E. olgae* came to Britain from northern Iran and Afghanistan. The flowers are usually pale pink but they can be white with a yellow base and are arranged on a spike between 70 and 120cm (28 and 48in) tall. Late-flowering, and considered by some to be the most beautiful species, it was named after Olga, the wife of Alexei Fedechenko, a Russian botanist who did extensive work on the plants of the region. Olga Fedechenko published several botanical works herself – the best known is her monograph of *Eremurus*.

Four years later, in 1885, *E. stenophyllus* was introduced to Britain from southwest Asia and has since become a garden favourite, with its clear yellow flowers. There are

flowers, which can be cup- or star-shaped, are arranged densely up the branchless stem – although in some species, the flowers are arranged more loosely, and this is sometimes the only obvious way of telling the species apart. Even before the flowers open, the great spires of buds attract attention and, when they are over, the effect is extended by the round seedpods, the size of marbles, bearing winged seeds – once described by the plantsman E A Bowles as 'minute greengages'.

There are over 40 species of eremurus, but only eight are in cultivation and some of these are more readily

ABOVE: *E. STENOPHYLLUS* **IS A GARDEN FAVOURITE AND HAS HAD THE MOST INFLUENCE ON OUR GARDEN HYBRIDS.**
OPPOSITE: CANDLES OF *E. X ISABELLINUS* 'CLEOPATRA' **AGAINST THE BRONZE FOLIAGE OF A PHORMIUM.**

at the end of the 19th century, and who is better remembered for his work on breeding irises. The Shelford hybrids vary in colour from green-white to yellow, bronze, orange and shades of pink and have flower stems that usually reach 1.5m (5ft) and flower in midsummer.

During the 1930s, the banker Sir Frederick Stern raised the *E.* × *isabellinus* Highdown hybrids at his chalk garden Highdown near Worthing in Sussex. Sir Frederick was introduced to eremurus by the plant collector Henry Elwes who, during his travels to the northern frontiers of India, the Himalayas and Asia Minor, collected eremurus knowing they would be a success in the sunny, well drained chalk conditions at Highdown. These hybrids tend to be orange to buff in colour such as 'Golden Torch', which has rich-yellow flowers, and 'Lady Falmouth', with its large orange-buff flowers, which received an AGM from the Royal Horticultural Society in 1938. Throughout the 1960s, a range of dwarf cultivars was produced such as 'Highdown Dwarf' and 'Golden Dwarf'.

Another well-known group of hybrids from the same cross is the *E.* × *isabellinus* Ruiter hybrids, raised by N C Ruiter between the 1950s and 1980s. The flower stems reach 2m (6½ft) in height and flower in midsummer. There are several brightly coloured cultivars such as 'Cleopatra' with its orange-red flowers, 'Sahara' with copper blooms and 'Obelisk' whose white flowers are tinged with green.

However, breeding eremurus hybrids has not just been confined to nurseries in Britain. In Holland, the firm of Van Tubergen became interested in eremurus when one of their collectors, A Kronenburg, despatched roots of *E. bucharicus* from Bukhara, Uzbekistan in 1904. Not as tall as some species, only reaching 80–100cm (32–40in), the flowers of this species are white or very pale pink and appear in early to midsummer, fairly loosely spread on the flower-spike. Once again, *E. stenophyllus* was instrumental in the breeding programme when, in 1910, the Van Tubergens crossed *E. stenophyllus* and *E. himalaicus*. This

two subspecies, *E. stenophyllus* subsp. *aurantiacus* and *E.* subsp. *stenophyllus*. The latter is grown commercially and is widely available. Previously known as *E. bungei*, it has bright yellow flowers, which turn orange-brown with age.

Eremurus stenophyllus has also had the greatest influence on the best-known of the garden hybrids. A partnership with *E. olgae* produced *E.* × *isabellinus*, which has flowers that appear in early to midsummer and which vary from white to yellow, bronze, orange and pink.

The *E.* × *isabellinus* Shelford hybrids were named after the Great Shelford garden belonging to Sir Michael Foster who was Professor of Physiology at Cambridge University

ABOVE: **THE ARCHITECTURAL SPIRES OF** *E. ROBUSTUS* **MAKE IT A MAGNIFICENT GARDEN PLANT.**

hybrid has pale yellow flowers on a stem of nearly 2.5m (8ft) high. The nursery also worked on the *E. × isabellinus* Shelford hybrids and raised many new colour forms that were first produced commercially in the late 1920s. However, the only cultivars that still appear to be in cultivation are 'Isobel' with pale yellow flowers and the rose-pink 'Rosalind'.

In the garden, eremurus makes a stunning effect when in bud and then later, when in flower. They are marvellous focal points and sustain the effect for several weeks during the season. The range of colours and height means that they complement many other plants around them. I grow them in front of large shrubs in my garden as they show up so well against a green background. Beneath, I have placed low-growing lavender and senecio, which has its top growth removed repeatedly to prevent it from becoming too tall and casting too much shade. Despite having been in cultivation for so long, eremurus was relatively little known until recent displays at the Royal Horticultural Society's Hampton Court Palace Flower Show and other gardening shows stimulated public interest. Indeed, gardeners have found that eremurus make a striking addition to the garden and once planted, they need very little attention.

ABOVE LEFT: *E. HIMALAICUS* PRODUCES MASSES OF WHITE FLOWERS ON TOWERING STEMS UP TO 2.5M (8FT) TALL.
ABOVE RIGHT: 'ROMANCE', ONE OF MANY EREMURUS HYBRIDS.

ABOVE: **WITH FIERY ORANGE BLOOMS,** *E. X ISABELLINUS* 'CLEOPATRA' **JUSTLY DESERVES ITS COMMON NAME OF DESERT CANDLE.**
OPPOSITE: *E. X ISABELLINUS* **RUITER HYBRIDS FROM THE WELL-KNOWN GROUP THAT PRODUCES BRIGHTLY COLOURED CULTIVARS.**

CULTIVATION

The leaves and flowers of eremurus grow from a central crown surrounded by fleshy roots. In temperate climes, they should be planted in autumn in well drained, gritty, fertile soil. The crown should sit just below the surface and the roots spread out around them. When planting a clump, the roots can overlap. An open, sunny spot is essential as the sun must reach the crown when it is resting after flowering and it is important that plants do not grow up to shade them in summer. While eremurus are perfectly hardy in temperate climates, some believe that they flower better after a cold winter although they dislike winter wet so the soil must be well drained. To improve drainage, put a layer of grit underneath the crown when planting. If necessary a loose covering of straw or bracken can be put over the crowns and a mulch over the roots, although care should be taken as this can become a haven for slugs.

Eremurus prefer alkaline soil and benefit from a feed of potash in the autumn. Do not move them more than necessary but, when a clump has built up and flowering has reduced, this may be necessary. The best method seems to be to lift the whole clump in one piece when dormant and dry it out. When dry, the soil can be shaken off and the roots teased apart for replanting. They are not suitable for pot culture, unless they are planted in a barrel, as there is not enough room to allow the roots to spread out. Apart from the occasional slug attacking the stem, eremurus do not suffer from pests and diseases.

PROPAGATION

Eremurus can be grown from fresh seeds, preferably sown as soon as they are ripe, but they usually take at least five or six years before they flower. They should be sown singly, or at least very thinly, in a sandy compost. They should be protected in a frame for two or three years to give them a chance to become decently sized plants, when they can be moved to their permanent positions. A simpler method, which is just as effective, is to let them multiply naturally and then to split the clump, although I tend to leave them alone until they stop flowering, which is usually when they are approximately ten years old. However, they can be increased by division when they are five years old.

Sedums

Sedums, sometimes known as stonecrops, are a wide-ranging genus that includes succulent annuals, evergreen and deciduous perennials and shrubs – although most cultivated sedums are perennials. They are widely distributed, most found in mountains of the northern hemisphere. Recognisable by their often fleshy, whorled leaves in shades ranging from apple-green to purple or bronze, many produce delicate, star-shaped flowers in summer and autumn. They are versatile plants – hardy species can be grown in temperate climates in a rock garden or at the front of a border, while more tender plants can be grown in a greenhouse or conservatory. The name sedum comes from the Latin *sedere*, to sit, and, as a child, I used to sit and marvel at the bright yellow cushions of *Sedum acre*. As much as I love snowdrops and hellebores in early spring, I have also, over many years, formed an equal affection for sedums.

In medieval England, *S. telephium* was picked on Midsummer Day and hung from cottage rafters – it was thought to keep distemper away. Sedums have also been used by herbalists throughout history. Their leaves have been used externally to soothe wounds, and have been taken internally as vermifuges. *Sedum acre*, called wallpepper by John Gerard in his famous *Herbal*, was used in Anglo Saxon times to treat gout and has also been used as a cure for scurvy, haemorrhoids and even venereal disease. Sedums have also been used as food. *Sedum reflexum* was probably introduced to Britain from Flanders as a salad crop. It was said to have a pleasant taste, and to be a good treatment for heartburn.

Today, I value sedums for their important contribution to garden design, in some cases providing interest for every month of the year. Few plants can do that – the majority, especially glamorous flowerers like oriental poppies, border irises and lilies, seldom last as long as a month. We draw in our breath with wonder, marvelling at silken or velvet

OPPOSITE: A CLOSE UP OF *SEDUM* 'BERTRAM ANDERSON'.

textures and the haunting beauty of rainbow colours, but all too soon they are gone – even sooner, if struck by unseasonal weather.

Not so with sedums – at least in my experience on light soil. Gardeners on heavy wet soil might find them liable to rot, or grow lank and leggy, since these are plants perfectly adapted to dry conditions, their fat, succulent leaves often coated with a protective waxy bloom. I am grateful to many different sedums, which thrive contentedly in my gravel garden, where the soil and subsoil is sand and gravel, the average rainfall is 510mm (20in), occasionally 405mm (16in), so drought is a way of life, not an occasional hazard. Although we often have no measurable rainfall during the height of summer, this area is not irrigated because we are experimenting to see which plants survive when hosepipes are banned.

Most sedums disappear in winter, except for the coffee-brown seedheads of the various forms of *S. telephium* subsp. *maximum*. Planted in bold groups (although one alone can be effective), among bergenias, helianthemums and bleached ornamental grasses, sedums add impressive deep tones among all the muted shades of winter, furnishing the area until they are cut down in early spring to make way for new growth emerging at ground level. As the soil warms, the sedums quickly form large, tidy mounds. They make a fine contrast for woolly lambs-ears and felted *Ballota pseudodictamnus*, while scillas and chionodoxas are seeded among them. In midsummer, I value their large, dome-shaped flowerbuds just as much as when they flood their space with colour – crowded platters of tiny, star-shaped flowers in different shades.

For late summer and autumn colour, try *S. spectabile*,

ABOVE LEFT: *S.* 'BERTRAM ANDERSON' **WITH SEA KALE,** *CRAMBE MARITIMA.* **ABOVE RIGHT:** *S. TELEPHIUM* SUBSP. *MAXIMUM* 'ATROPURPUREUM'.
OPPOSITE: *S. POPULIFOLIUM,* **WHICH BETH CHATTO THINKS IS UNDERRATED. SHE SUGGESTS PLANTING IT WITH MOUNDS OF SEMPERVIVUM.**

commonly known as the ice plant, a great attraction to bees and hoverflies. There are many cultivars now available. These include 'Brilliant', which has light green, slightly scalloped leaves and brilliant pink clusters of flowers. 'Meteor' has darker, rich purple flowers, while 'Iceberg' is pure white. Other well-known sedums are the cultivars 'Autumn Joy' – or more correctly 'Herbstfreude', as it was originally called when it was raised in Germany – and 'Ruby Glow' (AGM). 'Herbstfreude' is probably a hybrid between *S. spectabile* and *S. telephium*, with brick red flowers attracting clouds of butterflies. 'Ruby Glow' is a low-growing plant with greeny-purple leaves and star-shaped ruby-red flowers.

A fairly new introduction is *S. telephium* 'Matrona', which captivates most visitors with its fine presence and subtle colour scheme. It has dark, upstanding stems 60–75cm tall (2–2½ft), clothed with fleshy leaves, flushed purple and grey. In late summer it is topped with wide, flat heads of pale rose-pink flowers – a beautiful contrast. I have planted a group of these among *Allium hollandicum* to cover the bare soil left when the leaves of the allium have died down, so they fill the space well into autumn.

Yet another recent introduction has been *S. telephium* subsp. *ruprechtii*, a superb plant for any soil but a soggy one. It is a little smaller and more dense in form than 'Matrona', but with similar pewter-coloured foliage. It opens earlier than

ABOVE: *S. ACRE* 'AUREUM' **IS A GOOD SPECIES FOR THE ROCK GARDEN.**

'Matrona', producing surprisingly creamy-yellow flowers from pink buds, while maturing to reddish-brown seedheads. The whole plant fascinates me from spring until autumn.

Often overlooked – unfairly I think – is *S. populifolium* from Siberia. Unlike all other sedums I know, it makes a small, bushy plant of woody, many-branched stems, covered summer and winter with light green oval leaves with deeply cut edges. By late summer, these are swamped with loose clusters of white and soft-pink flowers. Place it carefully among modest neighbours, perhaps the very tiny sedums such as *S. spathulifolium* or *S. hispanicum* var. *minus* 'Aureum', or clustered mounds of sempervivum and maybe a blue grass such as *Festuca glauca* 'Elijah Blue'. By

chance I tucked a plant of *Diascia barbarae* 'Blackthorn Apricot' beside it and found the combination irresistible.

The extreme opposite of these sedums in form and habit are the species that are very small carpeters. In the wrong place, they can be a plague, smothering choice alpines. But adapted as they are to dry, rocky or stony situations they will grow and flourish where some alpines would fail dismally. The bright yellow flowers of *S. acre* can be found sitting on roof tiles, covering the tops of crumbly walls and scattered along dusty verges. It is perhaps too invasive in the garden but I still make space for *S. acre* 'Aureum' with its soft creamy-yellow leaves – from a distance they resemble lightly cooked pancakes tossed over dry gravelly soil.

Sedum dasyphyllum, from the Mediterranean region, is similar, forming carpets of short, wiry stems, holding dense tufts of tiny grey-green leaves that turn bright coral-red in dry weather. This is a delight when smothered with pale pink and white starry flowers. Equally arresting is *S. obtusatum* from North America. This has dense clusters of tiny fleshy leaves, which are bright green in winter, turning brilliant rusty-red in high summer, studded with yellow stars.

Sedum spathulifolium, again from rocky hillsides in North America, makes small rosettes of fleshy leaves, each the size and shape of a child's fingernail, packed close in low mounds. The leaves are deep plum, tinged whitish in summer or entirely grey in the case of *S. spathulifolium* 'Cape Blanco'. Being marble-smooth, with such attractive foliage, I could do without the bright yellow flowers. There are heaps more! Some I have lost, but writing this I am determined to find them again. Others I must leave out for lack of space. And yet others are classified by some botanists under different genera – some crassula, for example, are very similar. If you are looking for further inspiration, I recommend reading the late Will Ingwersen's *Manual of Alpine Plants* (1991).

ABOVE: *S. SPECTABILE* 'ICEBERG', **A STUNNING PLANT WITH PALE GREEN LEAVES AND PURE WHITE FLOWERS APPEARING IN LATE SUMMER.**

ABOVE: **FROM LATE SUMMER INTO EARLY WINTER,** *S. SPECTABILE* 'HERBSTFREUDE' **PROMISES A FINE DISPLAY.**
OPPOSITE: *S. SPATHULIFOLIUM* 'PURPUREUM' (AGM) **HAS YELLOW FLOWERS IN SUMMER.**

CULTIVATION

Sedums are easily grown in full sun in most soils except those that become excessively wet. They are invaluable in areas of low rainfall, being naturally adapted to dry conditions, and most will grow easily in rocky or stony situations. Some of the more vigorous species will tolerate light shade.

PROPAGATION

Perennial sedums are very easy to propagate from softwood cuttings in early summer – many of them will grow from a single leaf if it is removed with care. Insert cuttings into a porous, sandy or gritty compost and keep out of full sun. Water after a week or so. Few people attempt to grow perennial sedums from seed, since it is much easier to grow them from cuttings.

PESTS AND DISEASES

As far as pests and diseases go, hot, dry summers encourage the proliferation of vine-weevil – little black beetles whose horrible cream-coloured, brown-headed maggots eat the sedum roots. No safe or reliable insecticide is as yet freely available. The only efficient relief comes from organo-phosphates, which are very unhealthy to handle. In the garden we dig up infected plants, wash the remaining roots well and replant in fresh soil. Sedums also suffer from caterpillar damage. Cobweb-wrapped bundles appear among the flower stems, filled with caterpillars that defoliate the plants if not removed by hand. A local entomologist has become very excited, telling us they are the progeny of a rare moth called *Ypononenta sedella*.

SHOW STOPPERS

3

Oriental poppies

Those of us who grew up in the landscape of suburban Britain during the 1950s and 1960s know the ubiquitous oriental poppy only too well. Along with red-hot pokers, they seemed to be the mainstay of every front garden. Memories of tatty clumps of coarse leaves, and those fleeting bright orange or scarlet flowers, may go some way to explaining why the plant has been out of favour recently. But *Papaver orientale* (the name refers to its origins in eastern Europe and western Asia) is now enjoying a revival in popularity. New varieties that manage to bring demureness and modesty to a usually flamboyant plant are appearing at an astonishing rate (with many coming from Germany and Holland), while old sturdy and longer-flowering varieties are being rediscovered. Combine this wide choice with straightforward cultivation (even in poor soils), and it's clear why gardeners are appreciating the brilliance and exuberance of oriental poppies in the garden once again.

The heyday of the oriental poppy in Britain was at the beginning of the 20th century. The Edwardian nurseryman, Amos Perry, bred many new varieties at his nurseries in Winchmore Hill and Enfield and among his introductions were the deep salmon flowers of 'Queen Alexandra', which made a good cut flower, and the pale orange-pink of 'Mrs Perry'. Unfortunately, the soft pink 'Lord Lambourne', which he introduced in 1920 (and 15 years later was recommended as one of the best garden plants by *Gardener's Chronicle*), seems to have disappeared from cultivation. Among gardeners of the time, the most popular of his varieties was 'Perry's White'. Its large grey-white flowers, with a deep purple blotch on each petal, had the Royal Horticultural Society's Floral Committee of 1912 in raptures. In a display of unanimity – rare in the RHS at that time – there was no dissension about its AGM.

There is an ephemeral quality to oriental poppies – in some cultivars, the flowers only last for a day or two,

PREVIOUS PAGE: *GERANIUM X MAGNIFICUM.*
OPPOSITE: *PAPAVER ORIENTALE* GOLIATH GROUP 'BEAUTY OF LIVERMERE' **IN ALL ITS SUMPTUOUS GLORY.**

depending on the weather – but they are floriferous plants and produce many blooms during the early summer. Typically, each delicate, tissue-paper petal has a dark centre that combines with the seedpod to produce a velvety-black eye. Cutting the plant back after flowering will usually produce a further flowering in early autumn and, although it is never as profuse as the first, the second flush serves as a nostalgic reminder of the heady days of early summer just as autumn closes in. Cutting back also solves the problem of unsightly foliage during the summer, as the plant has a tendency to die rather ungracefully. Unfortunately, in doing this, you lose the velvet-topped seedheads, which, although not as stately as the dried seedheads of the biennial poppies that stand sentinel in winter, coated in frost, do bring interest to the garden in late autumn and winter.

There are over 150 varieties of oriental poppy listed in the *RHS Plant Finder*. With a wide spectrum of both colour and style – crimped, ruffled or cut petals – choosing one for the garden is not an easy task.

The varieties with bright pillar-box red flowers are the most familiar – and the ones that have given the plant a bad press among the faint-hearted – but recently, adventurous designers and gardeners are daring to use the sumptuous reds of cultivars such as *P. orientale* Goliath Group 'Beauty of Livermere' in their planting plans – a tall and elegant plant that grows to a height of 1.2m (4ft). Plants offered for sale are often grown from seed, so make sure you are buying a good form. 'Beauty of Livermere' has good clear scarlet flowers, with large open blooms that add zing to any planting scheme. A massed planting of this cultivar in front of a long yew hedge is a wonderful sight. Perhaps the most spectacular red cultivar is 'Indian Chief'. Its big mahogany-red flowers have a solid appearance echoed in the sturdy stems that don't need staking. In my garden it flowers later than other

ABOVE LEFT: *P. ORIENTALE* 'CEDRIC MORRIS' – **'FULL OF CHARM AND ELEGANCE'. ABOVE RIGHT:** *P. ORIENTALE* 'KARINE' – **'LIKE A GEISHA IN A BORDELLO'.**
OPPOSITE: *P. ORIENTALE* 'PATTY'S PLUM' **MADE A METEORIC RISE TO FAME AFTER THE CHELSEA FLOWER SHOW IN 1999.**

cultivars, often continuing into midsummer if the weather is not too hot.

To really frighten the neighbours, you can't beat orange-flowered oriental poppies. As its name suggests, 'Orangeade Maison' is a sparkling bright orange, which we grow in front of a chocolate-leaved canna. When the poppy is in flower, the blooms of the canna are still a long way off, so there is little chance of a hideous colour clash. 'Beauty Queen' is a much softer shade of orange. A friend is growing it among the tall blue spires of *Anchusa azurea* 'Loddon Royalist', which sounds unlikely, but it looks stunning. And there is 'Picotée', a very distinctive cultivar

with a double row of white petals edged with orange. Some forms are more orange than white, but the true form should look as though the flowers have just been lightly dipped in orange dye.

The pastel shades of oriental poppies are less exhilarating but make equally imposing plants. The grey-pink flowers of 'Cedric Morris' have a central black eye and, as you would expect from a plant bearing the renowned plantsman's name, are full of charm and elegance. We grow it in the garden with *Onopordum acanthium*, which enhances the silver-grey tones in the flower, and the purple globes of both *Allium hollandicum*

ABOVE: TASTEFUL CONTRAST IN THE PAPERY BLOOMS OF *P. ORIENTALE* 'BLACK AND WHITE'.

'Perry's White' is still one of the best white-flowered oriental poppies – its dark purple markings fade to white, rather than contrasting sharply as they do in another popular white form, 'Black and White'. There are several new seed strains with white flowers too, such as 'Choir Boy' and 'Royal Wedding', with large flowers and slightly ruffled petals, but the size and shape of the flowers of both these cultivars can vary a great deal.

In Europe, nurseries are breeding many new varieties, but it was a chance seedling that recently captured gardeners' imaginations. Found growing on nursery-woman Patricia Marrow's compost heap, 'Patty's Plum' was rescued by plantsman Nori Pope, and subsequently caused a mini-mania, particularly after it was used to stunning effect in Carol Klein's Chelsea Flower Show garden in 1999. Gardening stories as wonderful as this are often apocryphal, but this one is true. The murky, deep purple-red flowers of 'Patty's Plum' fade (rather too quickly) to a shade of almost-brown. But it looks great against the silver foliage of cardoons such as *Cynara cardunculus*, which also mask its untidy foliage as the season progresses. The flowers can fade to an unattractive burnt-mahogany in strong sunlight, so deadhead them quickly or grow the plant in light shade. Several sports have been introduced, the best of which, 'Lilac Girl', is lighter in colour and doesn't fade as readily. Another good recent introduction is 'John Metcalf', with a double row of rounded, slightly ruffled salmon-pink flowers, selected from oriental poppies growing in plantsman Piet Oudolf's nursery in Holland. And from Germany comes 'Zuneigung', which has two layers of crimped salmon-pink petals that fade to a pale pink, giving an impression of two-toned flowers.

The oriental poppy lends gardens an *embarras de richesses*, without complicated growing requirements and, in the planting schemes of the fearless gardener, it can either add a touch of serene modesty or an exuberant shout of joy.

'Purple Sensation' and *A. cristophii*. I've also seen it growing very effectively with dark purple lupins. 'Raspberry Queen' is a deeper pink cultivar with crimped tissue paper petals and dark smudged eyes, which remind one of Dusty Springfield, while the salmon-pink petals of 'Forncett Summer' are irregularly cut, giving a frilled, shaggy look to the flower. Another soft-pink variety is the supremely elegant 'Karine'; its silky-smooth petals form a perfectly rounded shallow saucer – the antithesis of the big and blowsy. Seeing 'Karine' growing among other oriental poppies at our nursery, a visitor likened it to a geisha in a bordello.

ABOVE: *P. ORIENTALE* GOLIATH GROUP 'BEAUTY OF LIVERMERE' **EXTENDS ITS STUNNING DISPLAY INTO MIDSUMMER.**

ABOVE: A PERFECT EXAMPLE OF *P. ORIENTALE* 'PICOTÉE'.
OPPOSITE: THE SHAGGY PETALS OF *P. ORIENTALE* 'FORNCETT SUMMER'.

PROPAGATION

It is extremely easy to raise your favourite oriental poppy cultivars by taking root cuttings. This can be done at any time of year, but cuttings are traditionally taken in early autumn. Simply cut a piece of root, about the thickness of a pencil, into 5cm (2in) long pieces. Lay these in a seed tray and cover with a layer of compost and horticultural grit (propagating poppies isn't rocket science; any well drained compost will do). Label the tray with the name of the variety and water well – do not allow the compost to dry out. When the first shoots push through the compost, try not to get over-excited as the root cutting will often send up a shoot before producing any real roots of its own. Bide your time and only pot up the cuttings when you are sure they have rooted – look at the underside of the tray for a telltale curl of root appearing through a draining hole.

CULTIVATION

Beth and Andrew Chatto's dictum – that you need only look at how a plant grows in the wild to understand how to treat it in the garden – has now become the mantra of every good gardener. *Papaver orientale* originates in southern Caucasus, Armenia and eastern Turkey where it grows in sunny sites on poor rocky soil and in meadows on thin soil (which makes it easy to please). However, oriental poppies will not tolerate heavy wet clay, which causes the crown of the plant to rot away. Otherwise, they are very robust plants and are not prone to any particular pests or diseases.

After flowering, the foliage dies away and looks ugly so it's best either to cut the plant back to the ground or position other plants close to it so that they grow over and hide the dying foliage. Gertrude Jekyll used both the scrambling perennial sweet pea, *Lathyrus latifolius*, and gypsophila to this effect. Annuals or tender perennials can also be bedded out after the poppy's foliage has been removed.

A less endearing feature of the plant is the quantity of seed it produces and the resulting seedlings, not very many of which produce something as wonderful as 'Patty's Plum'. If you want to keep out rogue plants, remove the seedheads before they cross-pollinate. The plant's ability to withstand being cut back makes the oriental poppy ideal for planting in perennial meadows.

Unfortunately, because they send out long, deep roots, like many perennials, oriental poppies are not suitable for growing in pots.

Geraniums

With their informal looks and tolerant nature, geraniums have a special place in gardeners' affections. Few other groups of plants require so little maintenance and are quite so versatile, easy-going and quick to establish. This may account for the increased interest in the geranium family since the 1970s.

Many species and cultivars not only smother weeds remarkably well but provide good ground cover in a great variety of situations. Yet our Victorian and Edwardian ancestors, who experimented enthusiastically with an enormous range of plants, ignored them almost completely. Perhaps they were just a little too wild in habit, and not quite showy enough.

A front-page article in an 1881 issue of *Gardening* magazine praised their virtues but referred to them as being 'encountered only in botanical collections'. European species such *Geranium phaeum* and *G. versicolor* were certainly known to early writers such as John Gerard and John Parkinson, the plants having been introduced into cultivation in Britain in the 16th and 17th centuries. The only species with a wide herbal use was the powerfully scented *G. robertianum*, recommended for a large number of conditions, including gout.

Geraniums, however colourful, always have that 'wildflower' look. This may have something to do with having a high proportion of leaf to flower, but this 'look' is probably the reason for their popularity today. The informality of cottage gardens and wildflower plantings are the perfect setting for their somewhat bucolic good looks.

The interest in hardy geraniums has gone hand in hand with the revival of old shrub roses, and the two do complement each other. The traditional rose bed, an ugly monoculture of naked stems amidst bare soil, has given way to mixed plantings where herbaceous perennials and other shrubs are grown alongside roses. Geraniums are almost tailor-made for this situation, flowering in early

OPPOSITE: **THE RAUCOUS** *GERANIUM PSILOSTEMON.*

a definite head start over many other perennials. They will flourish in meadow plantings with grasses, and alongside shrubs and other herbaceous plants, with almost no attention. In settings such as these, the natural growth habit of the plants can be fully appreciated, the long flowering stems often being supported by grasses and other plants, the flowers poking out over a wide radius among surrounding vegetation.

While geraniums make wonderful border plants, they are used to being supported by neighbouring plants. Before flowering, the neat hemispheres of bold leaves are an engaging sight in themselves, and quite magnificent when in full flower in early summer. It is after flowering that problems may arise.

Many of the taller species, especially those producing lush growth on fertile soils or in damp seasons, can collapse after flowering to produce an unsightly sprawling mess. This is the time to get out the shears and ruthlessly cut back the old growth to just above ground level. In about two weeks new growth will have sprouted, and in the case of many species, certainly the pink *G. endressii* types, flowering will start again in another month (albeit at a reduced pace) and continue until just after the first frosts of autumn.

It is the pink-flowered species and cultivars of the *G. endressii* group that make the best ground cover, especially if weeds are a problem; they are in the first rank of border plants too, given their habit of flowering recurrently, or even continuously, through the summer. They are among the fastest spreaders in the genus, with rhizomes that split easily to propagate new plants. Originally from the Pyrenees, *G. endressii* has a wide range of colour forms, from white through to a rich dark magenta. Closely related is *G. versicolor*, with charming pale pink flowers, which have darker veining and a lengthy flowering season. These two species have hybridised to produce the *G. × oxonianum* hybrids such as 'A. T. Johnson'

summer, at the same time as the roses. They are also the right height to provide an understorey that fills in the space around the rose stems.

Geraniums are also ideal plants for the increasingly popular genre of wild or ecosystem planting. The great majority are vigorous growers, able to establish remarkably quickly in all but the driest sites. Their ability and desire to grow at any temperature above freezing point gives them

ABOVE: *G. X ONONIANUM* 'CLARIDGE DRUCE' **WILL COMBAT MOST WEEDS IN AN EFFORT TO DISPLAY ITS ACID-PINK FLOWERS.**
OPPOSITE: *G. MACRORRHIZUM* 'CZAKOR' **IS A GOOD FILLER, HAPPILY SPREADING OUT EVEN IN DRY SOILS.**

and 'Rose Clair', all in various shades of pink, reaching 50cm (20in) in height and as much across in their second year. 'Winscombe' is neater, at around 30 × 40cm (12 × 16in), with a good show of flowers that gradually deepen in colour, giving a most attractive bicolour effect. One of the finest is 'Wargrave Pink', a deep salmony colour.

For those with really difficult places to fill, G. × *oxonianum* 'Claridge Druce' is the Rambo of the genus, with an ability to fight its way through all weeds this side of Japanese knotweed. Its rather crass pink flowers tend to scream for attention, although this can sometimes be a virtue. It grows to 80cm (32in) with a 1m (40in) spread. It

also seeds more freely than most other geraniums. New introductions like 'Hollywood', which is like G. *versicolor*, and the subtle pink 'Lady Moore', appear to have a similar constitution.

G. *macrorrhizum* is another strong spreader of similar size to G. *endressii* with good weed-smothering potential. Coming from the Mediterranean it copes well with drier soils, including lightly shaded areas around the edges of trees. There are a number of colour forms including the white 'Album', the pale pink 'Ingwersen's Variety' and 'Czakor', a dark magenta. They all flower in early spring to late summer, not repeating but at least staying tidier than

ABOVE LEFT: *G. PHAEUM,* **THE MOURNING WIDOW.**
ABOVE RIGHT: *G. PRATENSE* 'MRS KENDAL CLARK'.

the *endressii* types. The foliage has a very strong scent and can be used as a cat deterrent. Human reactions to the smell vary from the disgusted to the delighted.

Of all the geraniums, *G. psilostemon* (formerly *G. armenum*) is one of the most eye-catching – a voluptuous and raucous plant with dark-eyed magenta flowers on 1.2m (4ft) stems, from early to midsummer. Despite its colour it is not a difficult plant to place in the border as it consorts very well with paler flowers, especially slaty blues. It looks stunning next to *G. pratense* 'Mrs Kendall Clark' or *Campanula* 'Burghaltii', as well as later-flowering euphorbias such as *E. schillingii*. Several hybrids are now becoming available such as 'Patricia', useful for its smaller size.

Along with pinks, the other colour range that geraniums have to offer is blue-mauve. One of these is the British native *G. pratense*, common on chalky soils, with good-sized flowers on 80cm (32in) stems. 'Mrs Kendall Clark' is an especially lovely, pale slate-blue form.

The best known geranium in this colour range is *G. × magnificum*, which must also be the most commonly grown of the entire genus. Its reliable show of rich mauve flowers in early summer, tidy habit and easy propagation have made it one of those classic plants that are distributed through the plant stands at church fêtes. Its only fault is its resolute failure to repeat flower, a characteristic shared by many similarly coloured species.

Geranium himalayense is a lot more generous with its flowers later in the season. It has large, deep blue-mauve flowers and leaves that turn a spectacular dark orange in the autumn. Growing to around 40cm (16in), it spreads by underground rhizomes, making it a useful carpeting variety with good weed-controlling abilities. With *G. pratense*, it has produced one of the best of the hybrids – 'Johnson's Blue', whose flowers really are dark blue rather than mauve, with attractive, finely divided leaves.

Related to *G. himalayense* is *G. clarkei*, one of the gems of the genus, with neat foliage and flower stems that take it up to 40cm (16in). 'Kashmir White' has the best white flowers of any geranium and a good solid spreading habit. 'Kashmir Pink' and 'Kashmir Purple' are selections that have a similar habit and large flowers.

One of the most outstanding 'blue' geraniums is the hybrid 'Spinners'. It is a tall plant with deeply cut leaves and a splendid blue-mauve flower that reveals its *clarkei* parentage. Much to the chagrin of nurserymen and their customers it is not a great spreader and, thus, slow to propagate.

One other blue deserving a mention is *G. wallichianum* 'Buxton's Variety', a selection from a usefully late-flowering species. The flowers are a soft blue-mauve with a much paler centre, intensifying as the temperature drops. Undoubtedly this is one of the loveliest geraniums but it is slightly tender, although established plants cope with cold winters better. It is not as easy to propagate as most, there being no sideshoots to conveniently take off, and the seed ripens at a time that is perfect for mice assembling their winter stores.

Last but not least is *G. phaeum*, the 'mourning widow', a vigorous and variable European species with mysterious maroon flowers in some forms. Most strains are really too insignificant for a place in the border, but the dark forms such as 'Lily Lovell' can be quite something, especially alongside yellow and orange geums and similarly dark *Euphorbia dulcis* 'Chameleon'.

Many new species, most from Asia, have been introduced over the last few decades and, for the first time, systematic hybridisation has been carried out. Whilst nurseries have been behind much of this, many of the best new hybrids come from Alan Bremner, an Orkney farmer and amateur breeder, resulting in the commercial availability of many good new plants, from vigorous wild garden plants down to much smaller trailing species for the front of the border, or even containers. This is definitely a genus to keep an eye on.

ABOVE: STOCKBEDS OF GERANIUMS AT COOMBLAND GARDENS.
OPPOSITE LEFT: *G. SANGUINEUM* 'MAX FREI'. **OPPOSITE RIGHT:** *G. MACRORRHIZUM* 'BEVAN'S VARIETY'.

CULTIVATION

Such is the good nature of the geranium that there is little to be said on cultivation. They thrive in any soil that never seriously dries out or is totally sodden, although they do better in a fertile soil or a moist one. They will grow well in either full sun or light shade. The best geraniums for shade are those with the paler flowers as they show up better in the gloom.

PESTS AND DISEASES

Pests and diseases are few. Geraniums are not top of the menu for slugs, although the odd caterpillar or rabbit nibble might not go unnoticed. More serious is the mildew that can affect *Geranium pratense* and its hybrids in dry years. Remedy by cutting back leaves to encourage fresh growth.

PROPAGATION

Propagation is usually carried out by dividing the rhizomes, anytime between autumn and spring. Any piece with a root and a bit of shoot is potentially a new plant. Those species that do not form clumps are best propagated by seed. Collecting seed is a painstaking procedure and needs to be done by hand just before the powerful spring mechanism shoots it into the great green yonder.

Once collected, the seed should be sown in spring when it will germinate well. The seed trays should be covered with a rodent-proof material as the seed is large enough to attract mice.

Crocosmias

For adventurous gardeners in temperate climates who yearn for hot, daring colour to add warmth to their late summer borders, crocosmias are the bulbs that beckon. Anyone who has travelled in the west of Britain or Ireland will have seen the fiery colours of the most common form of crocosmia spicing up banks and hedgerows from midsummer through to early autumn. This widespread and indestructible orange flower, often referred to as montbretia, is *Crocosmia × crocosmiiflora* – a vigorous and fertile hybrid between *C. aurea* and *C. pottsii*, raised in France in 1880 by the celebrated nurseryman Lemoine of Nancy, also famous for his breeding of lilacs and philadelphus. Today, this English cottage garden favourite has been superseded by larger-flowered hybrids, in colours ranging from pale yellow to deep red. These hybrids are also commonly referred to under the umbrella term of montbretia. Originally from South and East Africa, crocosmias thrive in warm, moist conditions, and are excellent grown in clumps to brighten up herbaceous borders. They are also very effective as cut flowers.

The word crocosmia means 'crocus-scented' – so called because the dry flowers smell of saffron (*Crocus sativus*). The first plants were brought back to England by early plant hunters like Masson, and in Victorian times they became popular as cut flowers. After the Second World War many of the old varieties disappeared – in 1948 only 15 varieties were mentioned in the *ABC of Bulbs and Corms* by W Shewell-Cooper. Old catalogues tantalise with descriptions of *C. × c.* 'E.A. Bowles' as 'a lovely shade of rose cardinal, pale crimson zone and yellow throat' and *C. × c.* 'James Coey', 'a rich dark red colour with pale orange centre'. The rich and famous did well in the early naming stakes, with at least eight queens, but only one king – *C.* 'Henry VIII', described as the largest of them all with flowers up to 12cm (5in) across, bright orange with dark markings. Sadly, it is now extinct.

OPPOSITE: THE GLOWING, EMBER-LIKE FLOWER SPIKES OF *CROCOSMIA X CROCOSMIIFLORA.*

Why so many of the early hybrids dwindled into obscurity isn't known, but severe winters and increasing labour costs after the Second World War must all have played a part in their demise. Still, for all the old hybrids that have disappeared into the mists of time, you can now find over 100 different crocosmias in the *RHS Plant Finder* and nurseryman Gary Dunlop has over 200 cultivars in his National Collection in Co. Down, Ireland.

The crocosmia genus is made up of six or seven species. The species themselves are generally of little ornamental value in the garden, except the best forms of *C. masoniorum* (AGM). This boasts long sprays of upward-facing, bright orange flowers, which bloom over a long period. *Crocosmia pottsii* has erect red flowers. *Crocosmia pearsei* has horizontal orange-red flowers with curiously kinked tubes. *Crocosmia paniculata* (formally *Curtonus paniculatus*) is a small-flowered species, which has a fuss of dark orange flowers from early to late summer, above dramatic sheaves of pleated fan-like leaves up to 1.5m (5ft) high. The rarer *C. aurea*, with large, glowing golden-yellow flowers, which dangle or face earthwards, provides the bloodline from which some of the boldest offspring arise, although it is reputedly more tender than any of the other species. It flowers in late summer in gardens that are well protected in winter.

Surprisingly, the fact that there are only a handful of wild crocosmia species did not deter plant breeders from

ABOVE: *C. MASONIORUM.*

OPPOSITE: THE LARGE-FLOWERED *C. X CROCOSMIIFLORA* 'STAR OF THE EAST'.

their quest. Over 50 hybrids were raised in France between 1880 and 1910 with names such as 'Soleil Couchant' and 'Etoile de Feu', 'Drap d'Or' and 'Bouquet Parfait', described as mixed orange and yellow. These are surely now found only in crocosmia heaven, as it appears they were all rather similar, and merged rapidly into a choking mass of leaves at the expense of the flowers.

Then, in about 1900, George Davidson was bitten by the crocosmia bug, and for the next decade he produced some of the largest flowered hybrids, a few of which are still with us today. Davidson was the head gardener at Westwick Hall, near Norwich, and his best efforts were later used by Sydney Morris at Earlham Hall, also near Norwich. These reached their peak at the end of the First World War and in the early 1920s, with well over 50 named cultivars, known as 'Earlham Giant Montbretias'. An early Earlham catalogue claimed

they were 'remarkable for their great size and beauty, many of the blooms measuring 3–4 inches in diameter… invaluable as cut flowers, also for giving masses of colour to the herbaceous borders in late summer and early autumn.'

The distinctive *C. × crocosmiiflora* 'Nimbus', with glowing orange flowers and a bold central ring of soft brick red, is one of the few Earlham hybrids still to be found. *C. × c.* 'Star of the East' (AGM), with the largest flowers of all, also came from Davidson's seedbed. This beauty, with luminous orange flowers more than 7cm (3in) in diameter, was found growing at Hidcote in Gloucestershire by Graham Stuart Thomas. It now grows well at the Royal Horticultural Soceity's garden at Rosemoor in Devon, living on a rich diet with plenty to drink.

There are many other early *C. × crocosmiiflora* hybrids to recommend. 'His Majesty' was awarded a First Class

ABOVE: *C. MASONIORUM* **HAS LONG SPRAYS OF BRIGHT ORANGE FLOWERS THAT BLOOM OVER A LONG PERIOD.**

green pleated leaves. 'Bressingham Blaze', 'Spitfire' and 'Vulcan' are further examples, all with upward-arching flowers of vivid orange-red.

Many of the cultivars are characterised by dark-coloured foliage, giving added interest before the flowers appear. The smoky bronze foliage of C. × crocosmiiflora 'Solfatare' (AGM) combines well with its apricot-yellow flowers to make this rather special. But it is not an easy plant to please, as it requires a rich diet with an extra duvet of leaves for winter protection. 'Solfatare' is one of the oldest cultivars available today, dating back to the 1880s, where it was first listed in the hybridiser Lemoine's catalogue. C. × crocosmiiflora 'Dusky Maiden' has perhaps the darkest foliage of all – a metallic bronzy hue. The buds are almost black and open to burnt orange brick with a primrose throat. C. 'Amberglow' is a real novelty, another hybrid from Alan Bloom. It has tomato-red flowers with a contrasting yellow throat, strongly dotted with dark red, and broad, dusky leaves. But the dark foliage also creates problems, making the plants more susceptible to scorching from the sun – which in turn increases the risk of infestation from the red spider mite.

Certificate by the RHS when it was raised in 1919. It is both large and vigorous, with glowing orange flowers, flushed red on the outside with a large yellow throat. The flowers can be as large as 7cm (3in) in diameter. 'Mrs Geoffrey Howard' is a rich tomato red on the outside, with orange inside, and a narrow yellow throat. A personal favourite is the late-flowering 'Emily McKenzie', raised in Northumberland in the 1950s – its distinctive, large, dark orange blooms have a pale eye surrounded by bold blood-red splashes.

More recently, the veteran plantsman Alan Bloom has developed hybrids from the large-flowered C. masoniorum and the more sturdy C. paniculata, the most popular being his giant, cardinal red C. 'Lucifer' (AGM), which is still going strong after 20 years. His C. 'Blacro' continues to be one of the best yellows – although the flowers are small, they last well and are held in elegant curving sprays above

Crocosmias bring colour to any herbaceous border and mix well with many plants. Hostas, which thrive in the same moist soil conditions as crocosmias, make a pleasing contrast, particularly the blue-green cultivars such as 'Blue Moon' or 'Blue Blush'. Going again for contrast, the deep blue of agapanthus works well with the warm tones of crocosmias. Look out for varieties such as 'Loch Hope' (AGM) or 'Midnight Blue'. The ubiquitous daylily, or hemerocallis, is another good companion, particularly the scarlet 'Red Joy' and 'Frans Hals', a lovely orange-red. Kniphofias can be grown behind crocosmias for a dramatic backdrop, doubling the impact of the fiery colours. Also natives of South Africa, they grow best in moist but well drained soil, in sun or partial shade. Try cultivars like K. 'Buttercup' and K. 'Mount Etna' for maximum impact.

ABOVE: THE APRICOT BLOOMS OF C. X CROCOSMIIFLORA 'SOLFATARE' ENHANCE THE BRONZE FOLIAGE.

ABOVE: C. 'JENNY BLOOM', **A HYBRID RAISED BY ALAN BLOOM – ONE OF THE BEST YELLOWS.**
OPPOSITE LEFT: THE EVER-POPULAR C. 'LUCIFER'. **OPPOSITE RIGHT:** C. X CROCOSMIIFLORA 'EMILY MCKENZIE'.

PROPAGATION

Crocosmias are victims of their own success, and colonise easily. The famous late Victorian gardener, the Reverend Wolley-Dod, wrote about growing montbretia in a Cheshire garden: 'To make them do well, the chief point is to keep them thin, so they must be divided.' Propagation is best by division and you should divide the clumps every third year or so. It is best to divide in mid-autumn and replant straight away into fresh soil. Remember to deadhead as seed can sometimes ripen, particularly on *Crocosmia* 'Lucifer'. The seedlings will invariably be hybrids and probably less good than the parents. You can also divide clumps in early spring – but make sure the plants are well watered beforehand, as drying, cold winds can damage them. Mulch well after planting, whether in autumn or spring.

CULTIVATION

In their native South Africa, crocosmias often grow in the shade of plantations and gullies, or near running water. They will not grow in dry, dusty soil or in cold, wet clay and die out fast if left to starve. If you do not have that delicious, bottom-less stone-free loam, dig in organic matter before planting to improve your lot. The larger-flowered hybrids require an even richer diet of well rotted manure. Like many plants from South Africa, crocosmias need an abundant supply of water during the summer – dryness at the root can be fatal. Particularly with the dark-leaved cultivars, watch out for sun-scorch. In the autumn, plant corms 7–10cm (3–4in) deep and cover with leaves or bracken as a safeguard. If you leave planting until spring, do so before the corms have begun to sprout too much. In the right conditions, they will multiply freely, sending out new corms in all directions.

PESTS AND DISEASES

Perhaps the crocosmia's worst pest is red spider mite. Good plant husbandry, vigilance and moisture all help to keep the problem at bay – so crocosmia collectors should pray for summer rain.

Kniphofias

Kniphofias, or red-hot pokers as they are commonly known, certainly aren't shy and retiring in habit. Grown for their tall, showy spikes of flowers from red to almost fluorescent orange, yellow or green, these perennials provoke mixed reactions but can have tremendous impact if thoughtfully sited.

The earliest illustration of a kniphofia appears in Van Stapel's *Theophrastii Ereii de Historia Plantarum*, printed in Amsterdam in 1644, under the name *Iris uvaria*. This species was deemed to have been introduced into cultivation in Britain, albeit under the name *Aloe uvaria*, by Francis Masson, the first professional plant collector employed by the Royal Botanic Gardens at Kew, in London. An early name for the genus was Tritoma, reflecting the nature of the leaves, folded along the length of the mid-line giving three hard edges. The current name was given in honour of Professor Johannes Hieronymus Kniphof of Erfurt, and was first published in 1794 but only taken up in 1843. The hybridisation of kniphofias began over a century ago though, initially, all the hybrids were within the typical orange-yellow colour range. The renowned plantsman, Max Lechtlin, of Baden-Baden in Germany, was one of the pioneers in hybridising the genus before the turn of the century. Hybridisation continued during the 20th century, when cultivars were raised and named by a number of nurseries in Britain and abroad.

Red-hot pokers, or torch lilies as they are sometimes known, are members of the *Asphodelaceae* family. Originating largely from South Africa, representatives of the genus are to be found the full length of the continent, with lone species also appearing in Yemen and Madagascar. Approximately 40 out of the 70 or so known species are currently listed in the *RHS Plant Finder*, as well as dozens of cultivars. Most species are evergreen, forming clumps of long broad foliage, but there are also some deciduous species that are generally smaller, with narrow, grass-like

OPPOSITE: *KNIPHOFIA UVARIA 'NOBILIS'*, **A TALL RED FORM THAT FLOWERS IN EARLY AUTUMN.**

Most gardeners will be familiar with the distinctive inflorescence of a kniphofia – a simple dense spike of narrow tubular flowers. While the most common colour combination is the ubiquitous orange-red and yellow, the colour palette is much wider than many people realise, covering everything from green and cream to amber and brown. The flowering period across the genus too, is much longer than generally thought, with some species starting to flower in mid-spring and some flowering in mid-winter.

There are five or six species that are hardy enough to perform well in a temperate climate and that have been tried and tested in cultivation. The first species to be introduced and cultivated in Europe in the 18th century, was *Kniphofia uvaria*. It makes a large bold clump, with scarlet flowers held about 1.5m (5ft) high, in autumn. There are several different forms of this species in cultivation today, under several different names. The most distinct form is the largest one, grown now under the name *K. u.* 'Nobilis', which flowers at over 1.8m (6ft) tall. All forms flower in autumn, and are quite hardy.

Other species that are often grown include two of the most substantial species which, unusually for the genus, form trunks or thick stems about 7cm (3in) in diameter. *Kniphofia northiae* was named after the much-travelled Victorian botanical artist, Marianne North, who brought a live plant back to the Royal Botanical Gardens at Kew. This evergreen species forms a short, stout vertical trunk up to about 1.2m (4ft), looking rather like a *Yucca gloriosa* but with broader and much softer leaves. It has the largest leaves of the genus, being up to 15cm (6in) wide and up to about 1.8m (6ft) long. At its peak, it is impressive, with an almost sub-tropical appearance, but the ends of its leaves tend to fray as they die back. The congested flower appears in late summer and is ochre-brown, opening cream.

The flower of *K. caulescens* is similar, but with brighter red flowers, maturing to a pale yellow above pale glaucous leaves. Its trunk soon leans over, growing along the top of

leaves. Most are hardy and easy to grow in temperate climates if given the right conditions. In their native habitats, kniphofias are often found in moist or boggy conditions – though as they usually grow in areas of summer rainfall, the plants may well have to survive rather drier conditions in their dormant season. Reflecting this, in cultivation, kniphofias require conditions that are free draining and thus not excessively wet in winter, but reasonably fertile and moisture retentive in summer. They are quite deep-rooted so they can obtain the moisture they require even if the surface of the soil is prone to drying out.

ABOVE: *K. ROOPERI,* WITH BARREL-SHAPED FLOWERS.
OPPOSITE: THE STRIKING LIME-GREEN CULTIVAR *K.* 'PERCY'S PRIDE'.

add colour in the garden so late in the season. Of similar size, colour and habit is *K. rooperi*, distinguished by its barrel-shaped flowers, which normally appear in mid-autumn. In the past it was often, and sometimes still is, wrongly grown under the cultivar name 'K. C. M. Prichard'.

In contrast, there are two deciduous and rather finer species that are commonly cultivated, both with narrow foliage: *K. triangularis* and *K. thomsonii* var. *snowdenii*. The former has thin, deciduous, vertical grass-like foliage, which seems to defy gravity, and soft orange or red flowers about 90cm (3ft) tall in late summer. The latter grows to about the same height, with slightly shorter and broader deciduous foliage and has distinctive soft orange flowers that are well spaced rather than being tightly clustered, giving the flowerhead a more ethereal appearance. It is reputedly tender, but has survived frosts of -10°C (14°F) in Ireland.

As well as the species mentioned above, there are plenty of good cultivars to choose from. Quite a few of the superior older cultivars have survived, including the well-known 'John Benary' and the straw-yellow 'Star of Baden-Baden', a veritable giant at 2m (6½ft) tall. As with so many other genera, not all plants offered under some of the old names are true, judging from current catalogue descriptions. In the circumstances it is best, where possible, to obtain plants based on appearance rather than name and description.

Space does not permit detailed descriptions of many of the cultivars, but a brief summary of some of the better ones, roughly grouped by colour, may serve to give a representative flavour of the range – and it will demonstrate the wide colour range available. Starting with the pale end of the spectrum, 'Maid of Orleans' is a distinctive and attractive plant with cream flowers opening pure white. Growing up to 1.2m (4ft), its flowers appear in late summer. The deciduous 'Modesta' also flowers in late summer with slightly shorter flower spikes, soft orange-brown in bud,

the ground, rooting as it goes, and repeatedly forking to form sizeable clumps. Two unnamed forms are in cultivation – the more usual autumn-flowering clone and the less common late-spring-flowering clone. It can make an impressive large-scale ground-cover plant, as can be seen at Mount Stewart Garden in County Down, Ireland, where a large shrub bed is edged with a swathe of this plant about 1.5m (5ft) deep and 15m (49ft) long. It is robust, hardy and easily grown and the glaucous foliage is an attractive feature in the garden even without the flowers.

Another species worth growing is *K. linearifolia*, which has broad, lush evergreen foliage. Its rather commonplace orange-yellow flowers can be forgiven since this species flowers in late autumn, and there are few competitors to

ABOVE: *K.* 'WREXHAM BUTTERCUP', **A ROBUST MIDSUMMER-FLOWERING CULTIVAR GROWING TO 1.2M (4FT).**

green in bud and open to a greenish cream, making a striking addition to a border.

In the typical colour range of orange-red opening yellow is 'Atlanta', the earliest of all kniphofias to flower, opening its flowers in 1.5m (5ft) stems in mid- to late spring. 'Royal Standard' (AGM) is distinctive with yellow tips to the buds, adding a touch of lightness to its rotund inflorescences. 'Fiery Fred' and 'Bee's Sunset' are two other good cultivars.

Among the reds, the centenarian 'John Benary' has few peers. It is a rich cherry red in bud and flower and makes an impressive display at just over 1.5m (5ft) with an elegant tapering flower spike in late summer. Flowering slightly later, and a little shorter but of equal calibre, is 'Samuel's Sensation', the flowers of which open slightly orange giving a subtle contrast to the flower. Of slightly greater stature but perhaps more orange-red in tone is 'Mount Etna' and, finally, rather smaller than all the others is the fairly recent introduction 'Nancy's Red'. Ending in the pink, the colour spectrum can be rounded off with a fairly recently introduced German cultivar 'Safranvogel', a late-summer flowerer that reaches about 90cm (3ft) in height.

Kniphofias provide a good vertical accent in the garden when they are in flower. The larger or more robust species or cultivars can be used as specimen plants, with clumps grown on their own, while the medium and smaller plants are well suited to a mixed or herbaceous border and can also be grown in large pots or tubs. The few species and cultivars mentioned above are but a small sample of the range available – there are many other worthwhile species and cultivars. Mixed, seed-raised kniphofias are widely available, and may well be as good or better than some of the named forms, so it is well worth looking for good forms when they are in flower. The range of plants available is such that there are bound to be plants of suitable size for every situation, and colours to suit every taste and colour scheme.

opening white. 'Strawberries and Cream' is similar but coral red in bud. Other slightly larger and more robust cultivars to look out for in this category are 'Toffee Nosed' and 'Cobra' (orange-brown opening to cream) and 'Notung' (a rich orange bronze in bud, opening pure white).

There are many yellow pokers ranging from the diminutive and pale yellow 'Little Maid' (about 60cm/2ft tall) to the much larger 'Bee's Lemon', flowering at about 1.2m (4ft). A similar pair of cultivars of a richer chrome yellow are the dainty late-flowering 'Brimstone' and the earlier 'Wrexham Buttercup' – both are robust plants flowering at about 1.2m (4ft). All are green in bud. There are two similar so-called 'green' pokers that flower at about the same height: 'Green Jade' and 'Percy's Pride'. Both are

ABOVE: THE DISTINCTIVE *K. THOMSONII* VAR. *SNOWDENII,* WHICH HAS SPARSE, RATHER THAN TIGHTLY CLUSTERED FLOWERS.

ABOVE: **A LARGE CLUMP OF** K. 'LITTLE MAID'. **IT IS ONE OF THE SHORTER CULTIVARS, GROWING TO 60CM (2FT), AND FLOWERS IN LATE SUMMER AND EARLY AUTUMN. OPPOSITE:** K. 'STRAWBERRIES AND CREAM'.

CULTIVATION

Like many other plants, kniphofias are best grown in a fertile, moisture-retentive soil. If they get too dry, they become slow-growing and shy to flower. Also, they are rich feeders and can deteriorate in impoverished conditions. Grow in full sun for the best results, although they will survive in light shade. In wetter areas, it is best to tidy up and remove old foliage in autumn. Kniphofias are generally reasonably long-lived, though it is best to divide or transplant them every few years. If left too long, they can deteriorate and become shy to flower. Again, this is more important in wetter conditions, as large clumps of evergreen foliage will tend to rot over the winter.

PROPAGATION

Kniphofias are easily propagated by division (though some plants are slow to make offsets naturally), and this can be carried out at almost any time of year, though spring is probably the best time. New plants can be readily raised from seed, though cultivars will certainly not come true – interesting and dramatic variations may result. Seed will germinate satisfactorily outside in the open ground in early summer, as sporadic self-sown seedlings testify. However, for best results seed can be sown indoors in spring in any compost designed for growing seeds. The seeds should be thinly sown, lightly covered and kept moist. The seedlings can be pricked out into separate pots when about 5cm (2in) tall, or even planted directly out into the open ground, to grow on.

PESTS AND DISEASES

Kniphofias are relatively untroubled by pests. Although the foliage of the broad evergreen plants provides an ideal home for slugs and snails, they seem to respect their comfortable habitat and, thankfully, leave the foliage alone. Kniphofias can, however, suffer devastation from the fungus *Helicobasidium purpureum*, more commonly known as violet root rot. One treatment, suggested by Bressingham Gardens in Norfolk, where the disease was quite a problem for a time, is to dust the roots with a fungicide such as Captan before planting. The soil should be treated one week before planting out with a soil sterilising agent.

Monardas

Monardas are sun-loving plants that hail from North America. A few years ago, these colourful and aromatic plants – mostly perennials – with their long-flowering red, pink or purple clustered flowers and tall, willowy stems, were well and truly out of fashion; recent breeding work, and a change in gardening fashion, are now restoring the monarda to its rightful place as one of the summer's most rewarding plants. Around eight species are in cultivation today, although it is the hybrids derived from crossing two species, the scarlet *Monarda didyma* and the mauve-pink *M. fistulosa* that are the ones commonly seen. Worth growing in any case, it is their late summer flowering that makes these plants so valuable.

Both *M. didyma* and *M. fistulosa* grow in the wild in North America. *Monarda didyma* was used in the 18th century as a tea in the vicinity of Lake Oswego in New York State. It is also known as bee balm. *Monarda fistulosa* is known as wild bergamot, a name that comes from the similarity of the smell to that of the bergamot orange used to flavour Earl Grey tea. Both have a richly minty aroma, typical of the mint family, Labiatiae, to which they belong, and this marked them out for the attention of herbalists. In the 17th and 18th centuries, the plants were used to cure worms and heal burns, while 19th-century herbalists recommended their use in cases of fevers, stomach cramps and headaches. *M. didyma* was discovered by the American botanist, John Bartram, around 1850, who subsequently introduced it to Britain.

These two species are not often seen in cultivation – other than in prairie-restoration projects in the States – because their hybrids and named selections are superior as garden plants. Hybrids and cultivars have been raised by various nurseries over the course of this century. Of the earlier selections, the pale pink 'Beauty of Cobham' (AGM) has a particularly fine reputation, with distinctive purply green leaves. Another good pink is 'Croftway Pink' (AGM), which came into cultivation in the 1930s, while

OPPOSITE: *MONARDA* 'CAMBRIDGE SCARLET', **ONE OF THE OLDER VARIETIES THAT IS STILL GROWN WIDELY TODAY.**

'Prärienacht', or 'Prairie Night', has deep lilac flowers with greeny-red tinged bracts. Finally, the well-known 'Cambridge Scarlet' (AGM), with rich, brilliant red flowers, is still one of the favourites widely grown today.

Most monardas cultivated these days are perennials, but there are exceptions to the rule. *Monarda punctata*, for example, grown for its striking pink calyxes and finely dotted yellow flowers, is a biennial, and *M. citriodora* is an annual. 'Hartswood Wine' is a personal favourite.

A biennial, but easily raised from seed, its dramatic purple flowers are shot with red.

The new era for the monarda arrived when Piet Oudolf, the Dutch garden designer and plant breeder, decided to start breeding new varieties that were resistant to mildew, and which offered a wider variety of colour and size. With a starting point of 'Croftway Pink' and 'Cambridge Scarlet', he raised thousands of seedlings, then handed them over to a local farmer who grew them like a

ABOVE LEFT: *M. DIDYMA*. **ABOVE RIGHT:** *M.* 'SQUAW', **SIMILAR TO** *M.* 'CAMBRIDGE SCARLET' **BUT LESS PRONE TO MILDEW.**
OPPOSITE: *M.* 'BEAUTY OF COBHAM' **AMONG VERBASCUM AND NICOTIANA.**

field crop, leaving Piet to select those that both looked good and had no mildew. He made two sets of selections – the first, raised in 1988, was named after signs of the zodiac, and the second after the names of native American tribes.

Of those named after the zodiac, 'Pisces' (now more commonly known as 'Fishes') has been a particular success. Growing to about 90cm (3ft), it has delicate pink flowers with light green bracts around the whorls of flowers. 'Scorpion' or 'Scorpio' is taller, growing to 1.4m (4½ft), with purple-pink flowers and matching dark bracts. This one has the advantage of a long flowering season – it often flowers twice – lasting from midsummer to early autumn. The paler, but also tall-growing 'Aquarius' shares this useful characteristic, inherited from *M. fistulosa*. 'Libra' (also known as 'Balance') is bright pink, with browny pink bracts, and grows to about 1.2m (4ft).

The American tribes hybrids are distinct, in that most are noticeably taller than previous crosses, at around 1.5–1.9m (5–6¼ft), making them useful companions for the larger denizens of the perennial border like macleayas. 'Comanche' is pink with darker bracts, and can last well into early autumn. 'Mohawk' is deep lilac-pink with dark bracts, while 'Sioux' is white with a touch of pink, and light green bracts.

Another recent addition to the list of hybrids is 'Squaw', a fine cultivar from the species *M. didyma*, selected by the German plantsman Hans Simon. Growing to 1.2m (4ft), it is rather like the older 'Cambridge Scarlet', but much less prone to mildew.

Traditionally, monardas would have featured in the middle rank of the grand herbaceous border. Modern perennial planting involves a less tightly stage-managed display, which enables plants to be used in a more fluid and natural way. There is more room for the kind of plant that might have been dismissed as untidy by a previous generation of gardeners. Given that the mildew that afflicts monardas has now begun to mutate to overcome the resistance of the new varieties, this might be the best way to grow them, positioning them so that their lower stems are hidden from view.

Piet Oudolf, famous for the magnificence of his perennial borders, suggests mixing monardas with achillea, echinops, perovskia, phlox, salvia and veronica, the idea being that the shapes of their flowers contrast with and complement the distinctive whorls of the monarda. Their habit can perhaps best be appreciated if they are grown so that they rise up among more clump-forming, lower-growing perennials, such as *Salvia nemorosa* hybrids. Piet especially likes to mix them with grasses, and in this way they can be valued members of the border well into the winter, the stiff stems and neat whorls of their seedheads contrasting with the transparency and haziness of the seedheads of the grasses to provide architectural interest.

In an experimental planting I manage at Cowley Manor in Gloucestershire, we have successfully mixed monardas with other lovers of a slightly moist soil, such as *Persicaria amplexicaulis*, *Lythrum salicaria* (purple loosestrife) and macleayas. The greyish foliage of the latter consorts particularly well with the various pinks, reds and violets of the others. Native plant growers in North America use *M. fistulosa* as a colourful member of prairie restoration schemes, especially those that involve some trees, such as projects in former areas of savannah prairie where the occasional tree casts shade, which monardas tolerate better than most prairie plants.

Mildew is unfortunately part and parcel of the monarda – even in the wild they suffer from it – but the recently developed cultivars are becoming more mildew-resistant. Perhaps we should just learn to live with it, as Karl Foerster, the century's most influential perennial gardener, seemed to suggest when he affectionately called them the *mühlebürschen* – the equivalent of our expression 'dusty millers'.

ABOVE: THE PINK *M. 'COMANCHE'* **AND** *M. 'SIOUX'.*

ABOVE: *M.* 'SCORPION' **IS TALL GROWING AND OFTEN FLOWERS TWICE IN A SEASON.**
OPPOSITE LEFT: *M.* 'BALANCE' – **ONE OF THE MOST MILDEW-RESISTANT CULTIVARS. OPPOSITE RIGHT:** *M.* 'CROFTWAY PINK'.

CULTIVATION

Monardas are very easy plants, rapidly establishing themselves on any reasonably fertile soil in full sun or very light shade. The ground does not have to be moist, but they should not be planted if summer drought is a regular occurrence. Monardas have a tendency to grow outwards, leaving the central part of the plant to die away. This means that in the garden you either have to accept this willfulness, or divide and replant them every few years. Clay soils do seem to inhibit this mobility, although rather to the detriment of the plants. Mildew is an almost inevitable occurrence but, because of the widely recognised dangers of fungicides, I would not recommend spraying. Choose cultivars that are more mildew resistant.

PROPAGATION

Monardas are easy to propagate, particularly by division. They practically divide themselves in spring, as parent plants split into a number of separate clumps. They are also easily propagated from stem cuttings taken later on in the season, although the likelihood of rooting may diminish after midsummer. Select strong shoots whose first leaves have just unfolded and, using a sharp knife, trim off as close to the base as possible. Trim off the lower leaves of the cutting and dip in hormone rooting powder before inserting it in cutting compost. Water thoroughly before placing in a cold frame or propagator. Monardas can also be propagated from seed sown in containers in a cold frame, either in spring or autumn.

STRONG PERFORMERS

4

Siberian irises

Within the genus *Iris* exists a distinct group of species known as Siberian irises. The name derives from *Iris sibirica*, one of the stalwart species in the group and not, as one might think, from the plant's place of origin. In fact, Siberian irises have a broad geographical spread in the wild, from central Europe to Japan and Korea. Approximately ten species are in cultivation in Britain, as well as many cultivars, offering a wide choice of colour and form that should make them top of the list for a rock garden or open border.

Iris is a large and varied genus, ranging from the small, bulbous reticulata irises that flower in late winter to the tall bearded irises that grow from thick rhizomes and display their blooms in summer. Siberian irises form a distinct group within the genus, and are some of the easiest irises to cultivate given the right conditions. In the wild, they are often found in damp meadows or by lakes and streams, and these are the conditions they prefer in cultivation, ideally a stream bank, pond margin or herbaceous border in moist, humus-rich soil. They will tolerate drier sites but do best if provided with plenty of moisture in spring and summer.

Siberian irises are tall, slender plants, with graceful flowers held on slim, sometimes branched stems from late spring to midsummer in Britain. They form dense clumps of reed-like leaves that grow from thin, tough rhizomes with wiry roots. In autumn the leaves turn rusty brown and the plants die down for winter. Iris flowers are easily recognised: their distinctive shape is made up of three standards (upright petals) and three falls (drooping petals). The standards are usually erect, although they can be horizontal or even reflexed in some species. The falls extend outwards and their tips, called blades, droop down. The flowers of Siberian irises are generally 6–10cm (2½–4in) across and are elegant in appearance, with pendent falls that often have a wide, rounded blade.

It is from *I. sibirica* and *I. sanguinea* that the majority of

PREVIOUS PAGE: *IRIS SIBIRICA.*
OPPOSITE: **A BLACK FORM OF** *I. CHRYSOGRAPHES,* **A SMALL PLANT IDEAL FOR GROWING BY A STREAM OR POND.**

the Balkans and eastwards into southern Russia. The branched stems grow to 1.2m (4ft) and hold the violet-blue flowers well above the leaves. The plant now known as *I. sanguinea* was described in 1794 as *I. orientalis*. This name was commonly used until the 1950s but it had already been used for another plant, so *I. sanguinea*, the name given to it in 1811, is now accepted as correct. *Iris sanguinea* has bluish-purple flowers and leaves roughly the same length as the unbranched stems, which reach up to 75cm (2½ft) in height. It is found east of Lake Baikal in Russia and into China, Korea and Japan. In common with most of the Siberian irises, these two species have flowers with fine, dark veining on a paler background.

Like the species, the cultivars of *I. sibirica* and *I. sanguinea* can be grown in a variety of situations. I have seen them in rock and woodland gardens, as well as growing beside water. It is this adaptability and their tolerance of neglect, while reliably flowering year after year, that have contributed to their popularity. The oldest cultivars, such as the white-flowered 19th-century *I. sanguinea* 'Snow Queen', and *I. sibirica* 'Alba', are merely selected forms of these two species.

By 1900, only 17 cultivars of Siberian iris were recorded but, as the species hybridised, more forms were introduced in the first half of the 20th century. Interest in these plants has increased rapidly since the 1950s and now they are one of the most popular groups of irises. Today, both parents are commonly known for new cultivars and much breeding work is being carried out by iris growers, such as Dr Currier McEwen in the US and Jennifer Hewitt in Britain. The early cultivars have flowers similar in shape to the wild species, with narrow, erect standards and falls that droop down to display delicately patterned blades; the blue-purple *I. sibirica* 'Caesar', introduced in 1924, is a fine example of this flower type. Breeders of Siberian irises have gradually developed flower shapes over the years, with the most significant development being the introduction,

Siberian iris cultivars are derived – indeed *I. sibirica* is the species that gave this group its name. It was the first Siberian iris to be formally described, in 1753, by the Swedish botanist Carl Linnaeus. It was already well-known in cultivation, but as *Iris angustifolia media*. Linnaeus seemed to be under the impression that *I. sibirica* was native to Siberia, hence the name, but he must have confused it with reports of *I. sanguinea*, which does come from that part of the world. *Iris sibirica* grows naturally in central Europe and

ABOVE: A WILD FORM OF *I. SIBERICA* GROWING IN TURKEY.

OPPOSITE: THE UNRIVALLED *I. SIBIRICA* 'WHITE SWIRL', INTRODUCED IN 1957, IS STILL ONE OF THE BEST FORMS.

in 1957, of *I. sibirica* 'White Swirl' (AGM). This has almost horizontal, flared falls, giving the flowers a rounded shape, at the time a completely new feature in Siberian irises. Since then, most new cultivars have 'White Swirl' somewhere in their ancestry and the original is still one of the best white-flowered forms. In the 1960s, the British iris breeder, Marjorie Brummitt, used 'White Swirl' to produce a range of award-winning irises, including the pale blue 'Cambridge', the white 'Anniversary' and the deep blue 'Dreaming Spires'.

Today, there are over 1,000 registered *I. sibirica* cultivar names, with flower colour ranging predominantly from pale blue-violet to deep purple. There are no truly pink forms but the nearest include the pastel 'Pink Haze' and 'Dance Ballerina Dance'. 'Eric the Red' and 'Ewen' are both a reddish-violet. Some cultivars, such as 'Silver Edge', have a narrow silver border around the edge of the falls. In the 1970s, Currier McEwen, produced 'Butter and Sugar' (AGM), the first non-fading yellow cultivar. The standards of this plant are much paler than the falls. Descended from this is 'Butter and Cream', which is a deeper, more uniform yellow. Developments in flower shape have given rise to

ABOVE LEFT: *I. BULLEYANA* **GROWING IN THE WILD IN CHINA.**
ABOVE RIGHT: 'SILVER EDGE', **ONE OF THE MANY** *I. SIBIRICA* **CULTIVARS.**

plants with larger, more robust blooms, with wider standards and horizontal falls. Some cultivars, such as 'Ruffled Velvet' (AGM), have falls with a wavy or ruffled edge.

Breeding in Siberian irises has concentrated on crossing existing cultivars of *I. sibirica* and *I. sanguinea* to improve flower shape and produce new colours, while relatively little work has been carried out on the other species in the group. All native to China, with some straying into Northern India, Burma and Bhutan, they should be looked out for, because they make excellent garden plants.

Iris typhifolia is a recent introduction that is slowly becoming more widely grown and although discovered in Northern China in 1928, it wasn't grown in the West until the 1980s. It has particularly narrow leaves, only a few millimetres wide, which form stiff, spiky tufts, 70–100cm (28–40in) tall, topped by bluish-purple flowers. It is one of the earliest species to flower (I have seen it blooming in Britain in mid-spring). Like the other Siberian irises, it prefers a moist soil but I have grown it in a rock garden in full sun and it has thrived, despite the occasional dry spell.

The following species are less tolerant of drier conditions and some, like the giant of the group, *I. delavayi*, need an almost waterlogged soil. *Iris delavayi* has branched stems that can reach up to 1.5m (5ft). The large, attractive flowers, measuring 10cm (4in) across, are held well above the foliage, and are deep violet-blue with prominent white markings on the falls. This is a vigorous plant that creates a dramatic effect when in full bloom, with its brightly coloured flowers swaying gently in the breeze on tall, slender stems.

The two smallest species are *I. chrysographes* and *I. forrestii*. I find them to be the perfect size for growing beside a pool or stream, providing a good contrast to the low mounds and hummocks of alpines and small shrubs in a neighbouring rock garden. *Iris chrysographes* reaches around 45cm (1½ft) in height and has striking, deep purple flowers, delicately marked with gold lines at the centre of

each fall. Some plants have extremely dark flowers and are sold as black forms or under names like 'Black Knight' or 'Black Velvet'. Another form, *I. c.* var. *rubella*, has blooms the colour of red wine. *Iris forrestii* is even shorter, growing to 30–40cm (12–16in). The flowers are only 5–6cm (2–2½in) across and are pure yellow, with attractive brownish-purple marks on the falls. This is a beautiful plant but it often hybridises with *I. chrysographes*, resulting in plants with a purple tinge to the flowers.

Iris bulleyana was first described from cultivated stock in 1910, by W R Dykes, a renowned iris grower and author of *The Genus Iris* (1913). Dykes later suspected that his original material may have been a hybrid between *I. chrysographes* and *I. forrestii*, as seedlings from it were quite variable. However, wild populations have recently been found in southwest China and the seed introduced into cultivation. *Iris bulleyana* has flowers of a similar colour to *I. delavayi* but it is altogether a smaller plant, growing to around 60cm (2ft), though occasionally taller.

The remaining Siberian irises are less commonly grown, although most can be found in cultivation in the UK. *Iris wilsonii* is another yellow-flowered species. It is larger than *I. forrestii*, reaching 75cm (2½ft) tall, and sports paler yellow flowers. *Iris clarkei* is unique in the group in that it has solid rather than hollow flower stems. The flowers vary from mid-blue to dark bluish-purple, with white markings on the falls. *Iris dykesii* is a purple-flowered plant that is like a vigorous form of *I. chrysographes*. Finally, *I. phragmitetorum* has dark blue flowers but is rarely seen and as yet is not available to amateur gardeners.

Siberian irises are all fine garden plants. They look good anywhere, but particularly beside lakes and streams where their flowers will hover over the water. Even after flowering, the narrow, arching leaves make an attractive feature in a border. Most of the species can be found in specialist nurseries and many cultivars of *I. sibirica* are widely available.

ABOVE: THE UNUSUALLY COLOURED *I. SIBIRICA* 'BUTTER AND SUGAR'. **OPPOSITE TOP:** *I. SIBIRICA,* **ONE OF THE MOST COMMON SPECIES IN THE GROUP.**
OPPOSITE BOTTOM: THE DISTINCTIVE *I. SIBIRICA* 'ERIC THE RED' **WITH** *I. SIBIRICA* **IN THE BACKGROUND.**

CULTIVATION

Siberian irises are generally easy garden plants, tolerating a range of conditions and a fair amount of neglect. However, although some, such as *Iris sanguinea* and *I. sibirica* and its cultivars, can withstand relatively dry conditions, they will all do best if they receive plenty of moisture during spring and summer. The rhizomes should not be placed under water but in a position where their roots can grow into damp soil. They can be grown successfully in herbaceous borders if the soil is humus-rich. A mulch of well rotted manure or compost, applied in the winter, is also beneficial. They will grow in partial shade but planting in a sunny position will produce the best flowering display. The new leaves emerge in spring and remain green throughout the summer until late autumn when they die down. At this time the old brown foliage can be cut back at or near ground level, taking care not to damage any new shoots. Siberian irises can be grown in a variety of soils but they prefer a mildly acidic, heavy loam.

PROPAGATION

Siberian irises hybridise freely so the best way to increase your stock of a particular cultivar is by division. The dense clumps of rhizomes can be dug up, split with a spade into smaller portions and replanted 3–5cm (1¼–2in) deep. Alternatively, sections can be cut away from the main clump. Division is best carried out in late summer, before the plants have died down, allowing time for the divisions to establish themselves during the autumn.

If divided in early spring, care must be taken to provide them with ample moisture during their first summer. Siberian irises usually produce plenty of seeds. They should be sown in autumn in a standard seed mix and the pots placed in a cold frame or unheated glasshouse. After germination in spring, they can be pricked out and grown on until large enough to plant out. Offspring from the cultivars are likely to differ from the parent plant and the vast majority will be inferior. Breeding new forms takes time, skill and dedication but, as the earliest cultivars were the result of unplanned crosses, the process can be exciting and rewarding.

Cyclamen

Native to the Mediterranean, cyclamen were well-known to Greek writers and physicians as a cure for a variety of medical complaints. Today they are better known as winter house plants and, in the garden, cyclamen symbolise the onset of winter. From the 20 hardy species there is a myriad of forms available with a wide range of flower colours and leaf patterns. Not only that: cyclamen enthusiasts often claim that no month passes without a cyclamen species being in flower. This is true, although things are rather sparse around early and mid-summer when the last of the spring-flowering species meets the first of the autumnal batch. Nevertheless, it is a remarkable achievement for one fairly small genus.

The early Greek writers and physicians used cyclamen for a variety of purposes. Theophrastus recommended the juice from the tuber for dressing wounds and for treating boils. This multi-purpose herb also had its uses as a good-luck charm, both as an aphrodisiac and to encourage child-birth. Later herbalists were still convinced of its efficacy in treating skin complaints, or 'cutaneous eruptions', as Culpepper called them. By the 17th century, at least five species were being cultivated in European gardens. The word cyclamen is thought to be derived from the Greek *kyklos*, a circle, referring to the rounded tuber. A vernacular name for cyclamen is sowbread, which refers to the fact that pigs are known to be partial to the tubers.

Mention the word cyclamen and the majority of people will think of colourful winter house plants. Theatre- and cinemagoers might well remember Miss Jean Brodie disdainfully dismissing chrysanthemums as 'serviceable flowers' and florists' cyclamen probably deserve similar comment. They are showy, long-lasting pot plants serving a very useful purpose but they lack the grace, charm and interest of the wild species.

The origins of this 'serviceable' plant lie in *Cyclamen persicum*, confusingly not a native of Persia but of the

OPPOSITE: *CYCLAMEN COUM* **HAS DISTINCTIVE, ROUNDED LEAVES RANGING FROM PLAIN GREEN TO SILVER.**

the base of the petals, but it also comes in shades of pink, and there is great variation in the leaf patterns. It is this ability to vary and its winter-flowering habit that have led to the development of *C. persicum* as a popular house plant.

The hardier species of cyclamen have many devotees among hardy plant enthusiasts, to the extent that there is a society devoted to them, now 25 years old and with 1,600 members. It is the autumn- and winter-flowering species that make the best garden plants and, out of the 20 known species, there is none tougher or better loved than the ivy-leaved cyclamen *C. hederifolium*, which flowers from late summer to early winter. In the most familiar forms the leaves resemble ivy, but the variation in foliage is enormous. The colouring ranges from plain green to entirely silver and everything imaginable in the way of patterns and shapes from narrow arrowheads to broad and prominently lobed. The flower colour varies from pure white through to shades of pink and deep purple and they can be scented or unscented, creating endless possibilities. In the wild, in central and eastern Mediterranean, *C. hederifolium* usually prefers light shade, and in gardens it is never better than when seen in dappled sunlight under deciduous trees and shrubs. In Greece it is particularly common, as is *C. graecum*, the flowers of which are very similar. Both species bloom at about the same time, in autumn or early winter, and often grow alongside each other, although *C. graecum* does prefer more open situations among sun-baked limestone rocks. The leaves, however, are recognisably different – those of *C. graecum* usually have a finely toothed margin and a most beautiful range of light- and dark-zoned patterns, overlaid with a satin-like finish. Although fairly hardy, *C. graecum* does require plenty of sun to induce it to flower well, so it favours a hot sunny spot. Other autumnal species well worth trying are the small, pale pink or white *C. cilicium* from southern Turkey, the pink, coconut-scented *C. mirabile* and the intensely fragrant *C. cyprium*. Although

eastern Mediterranean – our botanical forbears did not always get things right. In its natural state, this is one of the most elegant of the species with long, narrow, twisted petals and a rich, sweet fragrance. Its habitat is rocky situations at low altitudes so, not surprisingly, it is one of the most tender cyclamen and is a lovely subject for the conservatory, flowering in the depths of winter. The commonest form is white with pink-to-red markings at

ABOVE: *C. REPANDUM* **IS THE SPECIES BEST SUITED TO OUTDOOR CULTIVATION.**
OPPOSITE: *C. REPANDUM* SUBSP. *PELOPONNESIACUM* **FROM GREECE.**

darker zone in the centre. Many cultivars have been named, such as 'Album', 'Maurice Dryden', which has silver leaves and white flowers, or 'Tilebarn Elizabeth' with its bicoloured flowers in two shades of pink, but the most enjoyable way of choosing is to visit a specialist nursery and make your selection there. Similar in appearance to *C. coum* is the clumsily named *C. trochopteranthum*, the name referring to the propeller-shaped flowers that are so appealing. Although this southwestern Turkish species is probably hardy in Britain and similar climates, it flowers more freely and in an unheated glasshouse.

For spring, the species best suited to outdoor cultivation is *C. repandum*. In a sheltered, semi-shaded spot it can be a delight, joining the later erythroniums and *Fritillaria meleagris* with its mid-spring display of slender, reddish-purple flowers. Very fragrant, this Italian and Greek species has white forms, or pink with darker markings at the base of the petals and silver-blotched leaves (*C. repandum* subsp. *peloponnesiacum*) or white with pink markings (*C. repandum* subsp. *rhodense*). Closely related are the small white-flowered Majorcan *C. balearicum* and the Cretan *C. creticum*, less hardy but fragrant and pleasing additions to a cosseted bulb collection under cover. Also very special and best protected from the elements are the rare Lebanese *C. libanoticum* and southern Turkish *C. pseudibericum*. The first has large, soft pink flowers with jagged carmine markings at their base, while those of the latter are dark purple with a blackish zone surrounding a white base.

The cyclamen season draws to a close in late spring or early summer but enthusiasts will not have to wait long before the fragrant *C. purpurascens* surprises by launching a few lilac-pink to reddish-purple flowers from midsummer onwards. Although from the European mountain ranges and very hardy, this is often the most difficult cyclamen to cultivate. Most importantly, though, it is a reminder that the start of the next cyclamen season is not far off.

the white flowers of this Cypriot species are never produced freely, they do appear over a long period and are worth having for their fragrance alone.

Cyclamen are never more valuable than in mid-winter and this is where the Turkish and Caucasian *C. coum* comes into its own. This tough little species has squat but colourful flowers, usually rich purple with a blackish stain at the base, although there are also pink and white forms. The distinctive, rounded leaves range from deep plain green to silver or pewter, frequently with a triangular

ABOVE: THE RARE *C. PSEUDIBERICUM* **FROM SOUTHERN TURKEY SHOULD BE PROTECTED FROM THE ELEMENTS.**

ABOVE: A CARPET OF *C. COUM.*

ABOVE: *C. HEDERIFOLIUM* GROWING WILD IN CRETE.

OPPOSITE: *C. HEDERIFOLIUM* IS ALSO KNOWN AS THE IVY-LEAVED CYCLAMEN.

CULTIVATION

The most important factor in the cultivation of cyclamen is to ensure that the soil is 'open', free-draining with plenty of air spaces. Nothing will kill cyclamen off more rapidly than compacted, waterlogged conditions. To achieve the ideal medium, the best additive is undoubtedly leaf mould or composted bark and, if it is a really heavy or fine silty soil, coarse grit or sharp sand. When growing cyclamen in pots for an alpine house or cold frame, the same factors apply and a loose, open potting mix is essential.

The hardiest species of cyclamen, *Cyclamen hederifolium* and *C. coum*, are best grown in partial shade, preferably under deciduous trees or shrubs in a leaf-mould-rich soil, although I have seen the former flourish under pine trees with a high canopy. In milder counties, the autumnal *C. cilicium* is perfectly hardy outdoors, as is the spring-flowering *C. repandum*. These are plants for slight shade whereas *C. graecum* needs a hot sunny spot in a rock garden or scree bed. Most of the others, and any special forms of the hardy ones, are best grown in pots in an alpine house or cold frame, with overnight frost protection for the more tender ones.

Given good growing conditions, cyclamen are very long lived. There are plenty of instances of *C. hederifolium* 50 years old or more, with tubers the size of soup bowls. Fortunately cyclamen have few pest and disease problems, although vine-weevil can be a worry.

PROPAGATION

The only practical method of propagation for cyclamen is from seed, since tubers do not produce offsets like bulbs. Growing from seed is extremely easy, and quick to produce results. The seedpods or capsules take months to ripen, so in summer keep an eye on them and, as soon as they are ripe, collect the sticky seeds or the ants will take them for their sugary casings, which they like to eat. Sow them soon after collection in pots, using the same compost as the parent plants, then cover them with fine grit. If sowing dried seeds, soak them overnight in water before sowing. Seeds should germinate during the following growing season, from autumn onwards, and flowering should occur within two to four years.

Gentians

If there is one flower that is instantly recognisable almost the world over, it must surely be the vivid blue gentian. The trumpet gentian, *Gentiana acaulis*, is perhaps the best-known species, but in fact this vast genus embraces over 200 species distributed throughout the cooler regions of the northern hemisphere, with colours ranging from blue to white and even yellow. You can find a gentian in flower almost all year round, with species that bloom in spring, summer and autumn readily available and easy to cultivate. I will begin with the autumn-flowering gentians, which are native to the Sino-Himalaya. In temperate climates, such as Britain's, in moist, cool conditions, they take centre stage in a border from late summer through to mid-autumn.

Of the autumn-flowering group, it is undoubtedly George Forrest's introduction, *G. sino-ornata*, that has contributed most significantly to horticulture. Discovered in Yunnan province in China in 1904, this superb species

was given an AGM by the Royal Horticultural Society in 1916 and it is still popular nearly a century later. With a spreading habit, the plant forms a central rosette from which many stolons (or runners) radiate. Solitary deep blue flowers with greeny-white stripes are borne on each stolon. Notable Sino-Himalayan species to look out for are *G. veitchiorum*, *G. farreri* and *G. ternifolia*. The following are some of my favourite cultivars, which are both strong in growth and free-flowering, as well as being generally available: *G. × macaulayi* 'Kingfisher' has sky-blue trumpets and orange-red anthers prior to pollination; *G. × stevenagensis* 'Bernardii' displays a mass of dark-blue trumpets at the end of the summer; and *G.* 'Inverleith' (AGM) is a prolific flowerer with striking deep-blue trumpets.

I will conclude the autumn section by highlighting a species that symbolises everything one could wish for in this all-embracing genus. *Gentiana farreri* was discovered in 1916 by Reginald Farrer, who described its colour as 'so

OPPOSITE: A CLOSE UP OF ONE OF THE AUTUMN-FLOWERING GENTIANS, WHICH PROVIDE INTENSE COLOUR IN A TROUGH OR BORDER FROM LATE SUMMER TO MID-AUTUMN.

to 7cm (3in) in height. I can recommend a few clones of *G. angustifolia* which, when planted in a rich, loamy soil, whether acid or alkaline, will grow and flower reliably well given full light and good drainage. A favourite is *G. angustifolia* Frei hybrid. This consistently produces a mass of stunning deep-blue trumpet flowers in spring. Similar to this are several angustifolia clones worth looking out for: 'Frohnleiten', 'Rannoch' and 'Krumrey', which I have found to be reliable in many British gardens. There is also a beautiful white form of this species, called *G. angustifolia alba*, which displays pure white flowers with green markings within the throat.

If the trumpet gentian epitomises the European alpine meadow, then the spring gentian, *G. verna*, is most associated with the rock garden. It was aptly described in glowing terms by 'the father of the rock garden', Reginald Farrer, as being 'more magnificent than tongue of man can tell'. It is found commonly in the Alps, as well as in a few protected sites in the limestones of nothern England and the Burren of Ireland. *Gentiana verna* subsp. *angulosa* is the variant most commonly encountered for sale. Recreating the natural beauty of the spring gentian in your garden is easy with one simple recipe – a trough.

I will move on now to a few species that are at their best in temperate climates, such as Britain's, in the summer months – some suitable for sun, some for woodland and some for marshy areas. *Gentiana septemfida*, distributed throughout Asia Minor and the Caucasus, is a reliable and hardy species. A sunny, well drained aspect is best for this plant, as it is one of the few species that will tolerate a measure of drying out. The plant forms a broad clump with spreading, leafy stems up to 30cm (1ft) in length. The flowers, which in the best forms are a lovely, clean dark blue, are carried in terminal clusters of up to eight blossoms – a fine sight in mid- to late summer. Taller-growing than *G. septemfida* is the superb *G. paradoxa* from Turkey and the west Caucasus, reaching about 40cm (16in)

luminous and intense a light azure that one blossom of it will blaze out at you among the grass on the other side of the valley'. This species can tolerate soil of a higher pH (more alkaline). I have found it performs well in a deep trough of free-draining, yet moisture-retentive, loamy soil. In its best forms, the flowers are pale-blue to turquoise, with long, needle-like foliage.

Moving on to the spring-flowering gentians, perhaps the best-known of all is the trumpet gentian, *G. acaulis*. Generally, in the wild this glorious plant is widely distributed, ranging from the Alps and Pyrenees through to the Carpathians and the Balkans. An evergreen, mat-forming perennial, it makes rosettes of leaves and has deep-blue, trumpet-like flowers. Similar in habit to *G. acaulis* is *G. angustifolia*, native to the southwestern Alps. This is a lime-tolerant plant with blue flowers borne on a stem up

ABOVE: THE SPRING-FLOWERING *G. ACAULIS,* THE TRUMPET GENTIAN.
OPPOSITE: ANOTHER SPRING FLOWERER, *G. VERNA,* WHICH FARRER DESCRIBED AS 'MORE MAGNIFICENT THAN TONGUE OF MAN CAN TELL'.

Also in the summer category we find a group of gentians native to Japan that grow in marshy areas. Distinctive because of its tall stature, G. *makinoi* is easy to accommodate in the garden given an acid soil that is not liable to dry out. Anyone who has enjoyed a trip to Japan in the late summer or autumn will not have escaped the sight of great bunches of this gentian being sold as cut flowers. Its leafy stem, up to 60cm (2ft) in height, provides yet another reason to grow G. *makinoi*. Terminal clusters of tubular pale blue flowers are produced from late summer to early autumn.

From even further afield, in New Zealand, comes G. *saxosa*, a gentian that shows more affinities with the related genus *Gentianella* because of its atypical gentian flowers. Best grown in a trough or raised bed in full sun, it needs protection in winter. In the right conditions, you will be rewarded with a bounteous supply of low-growing shiny leaves, covered in mid- to late summer with a mass of white flowers. Although there are a number of related species native to New Zealand, most of which are white-flowered, G. *saxosa* is consistently the best grower, propagated easily from seed.

in height. The large, deep blue flowers can be white inside the corolla and provide a fine show in the garden from late summer onwards. Both these species are easily raised from seed.

Another late-summer gentian is the willow gentian, G. *asclepiadea*, native to central and southern Europe. One of the few gentians suitable for a woodland garden, it has wonderful arching stems up to 60cm (2ft) in height, carrying many blue flowers held erect on one side of the stem. The flowers are bell-shaped and often purple-spotted within. This gentian associates admirably with ferns and astrantias, providing valuable colour in late summer. Some excellent forms of the willow gentian can be found in specialist nurseries, including the white G. *ascelpiadea* var. *alba*, a pink strain called 'Pink Cascade' and an improvement of the blue form called 'Knightshayes'. On the whole, G. *asclepiadea* is a rewarding species easily raised from seed sown soon after ripening.

When writing a profile on so large a genus, it is inevitable that some readers' favourites will have escaped mention. There are many wonderful species available, and a few more recent introductions bound to captivate the experienced grower. However, there is one other gentian I cannot end without mentioning. While working in Bavaria I frequently came across a beverage known as 'Enzian Schnapps', which has the blue trumpet gentian on its label. This potent drink is actually distilled from the roots of another, very distinct gentian – the tall-growing, yellow-flowered G. *lutea*. Pliny and Dioscorides tell stories of gentians being used in antiquity to cure the plague. My personal experience of the schnapps would certainly confirm a rapid recovery from ailments, whether real or imaginary!

ABOVE: A WHITE AUTUMN-FLOWERING GENTIAN.

ABOVE: *G. SINO-ORNATA*, A BEAUTIFUL, GARDEN-WORTHY SPECIES FROM CHINA, INTRODUCED BY GEORGE FORREST IN 1904.

ABOVE: *G. SAXOSA,* FROM NEW ZEALAND, WHICH FLOWERS IN MID- TO LATE SUMMER. OPPOSITE LEFT: *G. VERNA* 'ALBA', A WHITE GENTIAN IDEAL FOR THE ROCK GARDEN. OPPOSITE RIGHT: *G. MAKINOI,* FROM JAPAN, WHICH FLOWERS IN LATE SUMMER.

PROPAGATION

Most gentians are readily propagated from seed, which is widely available from seed suppliers. The autumn gentians may easily be propagated by division. This should take place in early spring from well established clumps at least three years old. It is important to do this when plants are moist and under stress. Having lifted the plant, shake the clump to loosen it. The thong-like roots can now be divided and replanted at least 15cm (6in) apart. It is important to water them in well.

PESTS AND DISEASES

I have not found gentians to be susceptible to any notable pests or diseases. However, *Gentiana verna* may be attacked by greenfly in spring, so look out for the curling leaves and treat with a suitable insecticide or soap and water spray.

CULTIVATION

Growing in troughs is the ideal cultivation technique for many gentians and is particularly recommended for *G. verna* 'Angulosa'. For a trough measuring 60 x 30 x 30cm (2 x 1 x 1ft), use up to 5cm (2in) of drainage material (broken slates or flat stones) in the bottom of the trough, covered by the same depth of coarse, well rotted compost rubbed through a sieve. Then add John Innes No. 2 mixed with a little gritty sand. In spring, plant eight or nine young gentians in the trough, and then water well. Firm down the compost and top-dress with grit. During the growing season, water well, and deadhead after flowering. After two years, the trough should be a mass of blue at the end of spring or in early summer.

Hydrangeas

In midsummer hydrangea blooms appear like watery reflections of their fellow woodlanders, the rhododendrons and azaleas.

Part of the charm of hydrangeas is their colouring, which is marvellously mutable. In the German cultivar *Hydrangea macrophylla* 'Altona', the flowers start out a vivid deep blue and gradually become a meld of titanium blues, reds and purples. A subtler transformation occurs in the sky-blue heads of *H.* 'Générale Vicomtesse de Vibraye'. In autumn it is as though the blooms have been hand-painted, colour washed sea-green and brushed with mauve.

Hydrangea-breeding reached a peak in France, Germany, Switzerland and Holland during the 50 years before the Second World War. The Japanese had been breeding hydrangeas for centuries but, during the 250-year ban on foreigners imposed in 1587, many plants remained undiscovered. But in the late 1700s, Carl Thunberg, a wily Swedish botanist working for a Dutch offshore trading post, circumvented the ban, sending his servants to the mainland on the pretext of collecting food for his goat. In the 1820s, German botanist Philipp von Siebold sent hydrangeas collected in Japan to French nurseries such as that of Messieurs Lemoine of Nancy, who used seed from *H. macrophylla* 'Mariesii' to produce three famous lacecaps: 'Mariesii Perfecta', 'Mariesii Grandiflora' and 'Mariesii Lilacina'. Messrs Mouillère of Vendôme then crossed 'Mariesii Grandiflora' with *H.* 'Rosea' resulting in two classics, 'Madame Emille Mouillère' and 'Générale Vicomtesse de Vibraye'. One of the first hydrangeas to be introduced into Britain from China in 1789 and named after its discoverer, Joseph Banks, was a globose-headed sport of the coastal species *H. maritima*. At around the same time a Chinese garden variety was brought into France and given the name 'Hortensia' after a certain notable lady. The hydrangea expert Michael Howarth-Booth later used this name to distinguish mop-headed *H. macrophylla*

OPPOSITE: *HYDRANGEA MACROPHYLLA 'QUADRICOLOR'*, **THE BEST VARIEGATED TYPE.**

surprisingly sub-tropical effect can be achieved.

Relatively few lacecaps are available today, but old varieties like *H. macrophylla* 'Mariesii Grandiflora' and 'Mariesii Perfecta' are still widely grown. One of the loveliest is the Japanese cultivar *H. macrophylla* 'Veitchii' whose large pure-white sepals are like butterfly wings encircling a cluster of bead-like buds. The best variegated hydrangea is 'Quadricolor', which was discovered by Michael Haworth-Booth growing in the famous Cornish garden of Tremeer. It is a bewitching sight, grouped beneath trees, with its tiers of white and lilac lacecap flowers and marbled leaves of grey and white edged in gold.

The low-growing *H. serrata* cultivars have a delicate, refined quality but, given shade, they are able to withstand substantially drier conditions than *H. macrophylla* types. The leaves are usually narrow and sharply pointed, and often develop dusky red and purple tones.

On markedly acid soil the sea-blue flowers of 'Bluebird' (AGM) make a striking contrast with this plant's red autumn foliage. 'Grayswood' has more reliable colouring and with a little sunlight the pearly-pink flowers mature deliciously. At one stage the ray florets look as though they have been individually dipped in raspberry coulis.

The Japanese *H. paniculata* and its forms are exceptionally hardy, and flowering on the new season's wood is virtually immune to frost damage. With species and cultivars like 'Kyushu' the distinctive cone-shaped panicles are composed mainly of tiny fertile flowers and there is only a scattering of larger sterile florets. More showy forms with the greater proportion of sterile flowers include 'Tardiva' with long tapering heads, and the luscious 'Grandiflora'. In 'Floribunda' and 'Grandiflora' the flowers become delicately blushed, whereas 'Unique' and 'Pink Diamond' (AGM) turn a deep velvet-rose. Flowering in mid-summer, the everlasting blooms often remain attractive well into late autumn with their fleeting amber-yellow

cultivars from the lacecaps.

The flowers of wild hydrangeas are made up of a mixture of large sterile or ray florets, which attract pollinating insects, and much smaller fertile or disc florets. In contrast, the flowers of the mop-headed hortensias (as they are called across Europe) are almost entirely composed of large ray florets. In the sheltered environs of a house, protected from late spring frosts, hortensias flower freely and can reach magnificent proportions. With their regular dome-shaped outline, lush dense foliage and round, papery heads, they form an easy association with the straight lines and angles of architecture. Curiously these 'man-made' shrubs also look well in a more natural setting, especially next to water and planted in groups of the same variety. When combined with large-leaved foliage specimens like *Gunnera manicata*, rodgersias and rheums, a

ABOVE: *H. ASPERA* SUBSP. *STRIGOSA* **NEEDS SPACE TO FLOURISH.**

OPPOSITE: *H. MACROPHYLLA* 'AYESHA' **IS UNUSUAL WITH ITS PALE BLUE BLOOMS THAT RESEMBLE THE LILAC.**

foliage colour an unexpected bonus.

One species rarely found in gardens is the prostrate-growing and somewhat tender *H. involucrata*. It is unique among hydrangeas in having an involucre, a covering of leafy bracts surrounding the developing inflorescence. The swollen peony-like buds crack open to reveal small lacecap heads of lilac and white. *Hydrangea involucrata* 'Hortensis' (AGM), an old, low-growing Japanese form grown in Britain since 1906, has frothy, double, creamy-pink flowers and its foliage is covered in bristle-like hairs.

Another curiosity is the oak-leaf hydrangea, *H. quercifolia*. Unusually for hydrangeas, this species from the United States prefers a warm, sunny aspect that allows the wood to ripen before winter. In midsummer, cool white panicles appear, followed in autumn by rich red and purple foliage tints. 'Snow Flake' is a showy double and 'Snow Queen' is

a superb selection with upright panicles. Also from the United States is *H. arborescens* and the naturally occurring form 'Grandiflora' (AGM), which produces large domed heads of creamy white flowers from midsummer. The cultivar 'Annabelle' (AGM) is superior and ideal for adding structure in a mixed border setting.

Hydrangea aspera Villosa Group (AGM) has handsome, velvety foliage and broad saucer-shaped heads of soft blue and lilac surrounded by pale pendent florets. The various forms can achieve tree-like proportions and the flowers are a magnet for bees and hoverflies attracted by the plentiful supply of nectar. To cover a large shady wall or trunk of a tree, use *H. anomala* subsp. *petiolaris*. It clings by aerial roots but needs support initially. Creamy white flowers in early summer are followed in autumn by a display of translucent yellow foliage.

ABOVE LEFT: *H. 'BLUE DECKLE'*, **A SERRATA TYPE, WHICH AGES WELL.**

ABOVE RIGHT: BLUE HORTENSIAS COMBINED WITH THE GIANT *GUNNERA MANICATA* CREATE AN ALMOST SUB-TROPICAL ATMOSPHERE.

ABOVE: **AGAPANTHUS AND** *H. PANICULATA* 'FLORIBUNDA' **IN SPRING.**

ABOVE: THE SHADE-LOVING CLIMBER, *H. ANOMALA* SUBSP. *PETIOLARIS.*
OPPOSITE: *H. ARBORESCENS* 'ANNABELLE'.

GETTING THE BLUES

With the exception of white, the colour of hydrangeas will vary considerably according to the type of soil. The blues are happiest on acid soil, while reds and pinks are at home in alkaline (try *Hydrangea macrophylla* 'Ami Pasquier' AGM, *H. macrophylla* 'Hamburg' and *H.* 'Preziosa'). The degree of blueness in the flower is governed by the amount of available aluminium and the capacity of a particular variety to take it up.

On obviously acid soil, below a pH of about 5.5, the lacecap *H. macrophylla* 'Mariesii Perfecta' turns an undiluted gentian but, on alkaline soil, 'Mariesii Perfecta' becomes pink. Blue-flowered cultivars may take a couple of years to settle in after planting or transplanting, during which time the blooms will invariably be shaded pink.

To turn a pink or red hydrangea true blue, use a proprietary blueing agent on acid or neutral soil. Or, make up your own with 7g (¼oz) of aluminium sulphate and 7g (¼oz) of sulphate of iron, dissolved in 4.6 litres (1 gallon) of water. Apply up to 9.2 litres (2 gallons) in spring and autumn, thoroughly soaking the soil around the plant. Too strong a solution will damage the plant. Dried blood is a good fertiliser, as it makes the colour more vivid. The variety should be one susceptible to turning blue, like *H. macrophylla* 'Benelux', *H. macrophylla* 'Enziandom' and *H. serrata* 'Blue Deckle'.

CULTIVATION

Until relatively recently, *H. macrophylla* cultivars were considered unsuitable for outdoor planting in temperate climates and were chiefly grown as pot plants. Plant hydrangeas in a deep, humus-rich soil, preferably acidic, that is not prone to drying out. Choose a sheltered, slightly shaded site (to prevent scorching and flower bleaching) and avoid frost pockets. Water young plants until established, mulch in spring and protect soft shoots from slug damage. Leave the old flowerheads on hortensias over winter as a protective covering and to allow complete reabsorption of stored aluminium. If frost damage occurs, carefully cut back dead wood in spring to just above a pair of living buds but do not hard-prune. The mass of new basal shoots which grows in response to the damage must be thinned to allow remaining shoots to ripen. On established plants, cut out a few of the oldest stems at ground level in late winter to encourage flowering. *Hydrangea paniculata* and *H. arborescens* varieties produce larger flowers if hard-pruned in spring, cutting back previous seasons' growth to about two buds from its origin. If chlorosis or yellowing of the leaves occur on limy soils, treat with sequestered iron. Late in the season botrytis, a disease that causes flowerheads to turn brown prematurely, is sometimes seen. Act immediately by removing individual florets to prevent further spread.

Snowdrops

Over the past century, a British plantsman's garden without snowdrops has become a rarity. Gardeners in temperate climates have come to appreciate the interest these elegant bulbs provide in colder months. Some species like *Galanthus reginae-olgae* flower as early as mid-autumn, and *G. platyphyllus* appears as late as the end of spring, but the main season for most of the 22 species and some 400 cultivars is from late winter to early spring. A true galanthophile will want the lot.

Galanthus is derived from the Greek *gala*, for milk, and *anthos*, for flower; while snowdrop originated from the 16th-century German *schneetropfen*, for pendant. The common snowdrop has been grown since earliest medieval times but, as the Linnean classification system is a relatively recent invention, it is hard to be sure what snowdrops were called in the past. The old herbals list them as *Leucoium bulbosum album*, or variations on this theme, meaning 'bulbous white violet', since they were considered a type of violet by the earliest cataloguers of plants.

The common snowdrop, *G. nivalis*, was known throughout Europe for centuries, but it was the arrival in Britain during the 1850s of *G. plicatus*, in the packs of soldiers returning from the Crimean War, that first fuelled British collectors' enthusiasm. Later flowering and generally taller than the common snowdrop, *G. plicatus* was found to grow well in shade or half-shade and to hybridise easily with other species. 'Straffan' was one of the earliest named hybrids, and probably descended from stock collected in the Crimea. Lord Clarina selected it and named it after his home in Co. Kildare. This late-blooming cultivar is of a purer white than most other cultivars, with distinctive green markings inside the flower. It almost always has two flowers to each bulb, one smaller and later-flowering, prolonging the flowering season.

The snowdrop soon became one of the most collectable of the Victorian plant hunters' finds, and the

OPPOSITE: *GALANTHUS* 'BENHALL BEAUTY', **FOUND BY JOHN GRAY AND E A BOWLES. IT WAS NAMED TO COMMEMORATE GRAY'S GARDEN NEAR SAXMUNDHAM IN SUFFOLK.**

– planting 'in the green', when the leaves are just dying back, is the most reliable way. The species *G. gracilis* (often called *G. graecus* in gardens), sometimes considered a subspecies of *G. elwesii*, is one of the finest of garden plants when happy.

The other notable late-19th-century introduction was *G. fosteri*, found by Sir Michael Foster in southern Turkey and native as far south as the Lebanon. Its southern origins mean is it one of the more tender snowdrops, best grown in pots or a bulb frame, for it needs heat in summer and hates wet winters. In 1883, *G. × allenii* arrived, sent to the nurseryman James Allen of Shepton Mallet, Somerset, among a consignment of bulbs from the Caucasus. Allen, one of the great Victorian snowdrop growers, believed it to be a hybrid; botanists today are still divided on the issue.

By 1891, snowdrop passion had taken firm hold and a specialist Royal Horticultural Society conference was held, where James Allen revealed his extensive hybridising work to an audience keen to try new cultivars and seedlings. Many of his creations are still grown today, including 'Magnet' (AGM) – which has long, semi-horizontal pedicels so that the flower hangs away from the stem. 'Robin Hood' and 'Merlin'; the latter two I consider among the most beautiful of single-flowered snowdrops. His most famous discover is 'Atkinsii' (AGM), which he named after James Atkins, a Gloucestershire gardener who grew snowdrops throughout his life and distributed this cultivar from plants in his Painswick garden. 'Atkinsii' is still widely available, and is rightly one of the mainstays of most snowdrop collections. It appears a month earlier than most variants of *G. nivalis*, and has long, shapely outer tepals with an arrow-shaped mark of a relatively acidic green on the inner segments. As flowering goes on, the plant grows taller until it is perfectly in balance with its long, flat leaves.

There are at least two variants of 'Atkinsii'. Firstly, 'Moccas' selected by the plantsman Percy Picton, which is said to be a very reliable variant without any of the

roll-call of those who gathered variants of *G. nivalis* and *G. plicatus* reads like a Who's Who of gardening. In the 1870s, *G. elwesii*, named after the great gardener and naturalist Henry Elwes, arrived from Turkey. This is one of the most variable of snowdrops, with convolute leaves that can be as wide as 2.5cm (1in) or more, but also very narrow. The flowers also vary enormously in their inner markings but frequently have a green arch around the notch of the inner segments and a separate marking at the base. This is rarely successfully grown from dry bulbs and – like all snowdrops

ABOVE: *G. NIVALIS* 'FLORE PLENO', **THE DOUBLE-FLOWERED COMMON SNOWDROP, HAS BEEN GROWN SINCE THE 18TH CENTURY.**

OPPOSITE: *G. ELWESII* **ARRIVED FROM TURKEY IN THE 1870S.**

tendency to mutate that can occur in the original. Secondly, 'Backhouse Atkinsii', named after the 19th-century bulb-breeder, R O Backhouse, which goes to the other extreme, and has totally freaky, malformed flowers.

The English plantsman, Edward Augustus Bowles (1865–1954), was another pillar of horticulture with an incredible eye for a new or different snowdrop. His book, *My Garden in Spring* (1914), fired the public's imagination with some of the first published writing on snowdrops. Bowles grew every snowdrop he could get his hands on, and many varieties are linked with his name: 'Benhall Beauty' is a tall slim hybrid that he discovered in the Suffolk garden of the plantsman John Gray, who is, himself, commemorated with a very early and large-flowering snowdrop; 'Ketton' is a sweet-scented snowdrop with two faint patches of green at the base of the inner segments, found by Bowles at Old

Ketton, Rutland, in 1948; and 'Augustus', selected in his own garden at Myddleton House, Middlesex, by a friend, Amy Doncaster, has wide leaves, striped in two shades of green, and relatively small flowers with crystalline outer segments that sparkle like snow.

Several snowdrops have a pronounced scent, the strongest of which is probably that of 'S. Arnott' (AGM). Introduced in the late 19th century by clergyman-gardener Samuel Arnott of Dumfries, it is an excellent garden plant that clumps up well and has a honeyed scent and globular, drop-like flowers in a shining white. *G. imperati* 'Ginns', a wild selection from this Italian species, is very similar to 'S. Arnott', and also a fine garden plant. 'Merlin' and a similar, but shorter cultivar, 'Tubby Merlin', are both sweet-scented. However, not all are cultivated for their scent alone – some say the variety 'William Thomson' smells of

ABOVE LEFT: THE LATE-FLOWERING DOUBLE *G.* 'CORDELIA'.

ABOVE RIGHT: *G.* 'ROBIN HOOD' IS ONE OF MARK BROWN'S FAVOURITE SINGLE SNOWDROPS.

antiseptic or even of lavatory cleaner! For sheer size of flower, 'Mighty Atom' is probably the best garden plant, but several similar seedlings masquerade under this name.

In the 1950s, there was a renewed surge of interest in snowdrops. In *Snowdrops and Snowflakes* (1956), Sir Frederick Stern listed 137 cultivars and 15 different species (the *RHS Plant Finder* lists 74 cultivars and 14 species currently available commercially). The double hybrid selections of H A Greatorex, a Norfolk plantsman, shine out from the many of the period. There is not much to choose between his various, named cultivars – all are of remarkable beauty, especially when one lifts up a flower and looks into the ruff of thick inner segments in tight rosette formation to see how well the white border shows up against the green. Some are less double than others, or have more green on the inner segments. My favourites are 'Hippolyta', probably the best cultivar, with neat, fully double, rounded flowers; 'Ophelia' and the ultra-rare 'White Swan', among the earliest to flower; 'Desdemona' and 'Cordelia'.

All of these cultivars are fairly easy to grow but this is not so of all snowdrops. The yellow *G. nivalis* 'Sandersii' (sometimes also listed as *G. n.* 'Lutescens') is often very difficult to grow successfully, and frequently dies out rapidly unless you give it the right growing conditions. The key to success may be the fact that this has naturalised in moisture-rich woodlands in Northumbria on acid soils. The green, double-flowered *G. nivalis* 'Boyd's Green Double', which looks like a green paint brush clogged with old paint, always provokes a strong reaction – its nickname is "the Old Green Horror", and you either like it or you don't. I know of only one garden where it is happy, and have never seen much of a 'flower' on it as it appears when the season is almost at an end.

Today the mania goes on. Snowdrops are still being selected and hybridised and collectors roam gardens far and wide in search of new forms. You might recognise the

true galanthophile by the way they examine snowdrop flowers, holding them upside-down to look up into the inner segments at the infinite variations in marking, the principal means of identifying one variety from another.

Among the most recent discoveries is 'Richard Ayres', found at Anglesey Abbey in Cambridgeshire and named after the head gardener. It is a striking double with convolute leaves, very early and with big flowers prettily marked on the inside. The cultivar 'Faringdon Double' flowers in early winter, with a smaller semi-double flower. Two of the newest singles are plicate (folded lengthwise, like a closed fan) cultivars: 'Wendy's Gold' with bright yellow inner segments and long, white drop tepals, and 'Cowhouse Green', which I found in a field in Buckinghamshire, with olive lines down the outer segments. Like so many excellent snowdrops, however, it is hard to obtain.

ABOVE: *G. NIVALIS* 'SANDERSII', **WITH YELLOW MARKINGS.**

ABOVE: G. 'JOHN GRAY', **DESCRIBED BY FREDERICK STERN AS THE FINEST EARLY SNOWDROP.**
OPPOSITE: A FINE PAIRING OF G. NIVALIS **AND** ERANTHIS HYEMALIS.

CULTIVATION

Most of the vast array of *Galanthus* cultivars are happy in woodland conditions and in an alkaline soil, in similar conditions to those enjoyed by hellebores and pulmonarias. Manure is not recommended – indeed some growers say it is positively harmful to snowdrops. I use old leaf mould as a mulch and, when planting, incorporate this into the ground with a general-purpose organic fertiliser (based on a seaweed, powdered rock and bonemeal mix that most organic suppliers stock). Snowdrop botrytis, which shows itself as a white mould at the base of the leaf, can be prevented by spraying with a systemic fungicide; once the fungus has appeared, the only solution is to destroy the infected foliage, lift the bulbs and wash them clean, then treat them with the fungicide. Root grubs should be sprayed with a systemic insecticide. Slugs are not really a problem because their predators live in the leafy soils that snowdrops also love, but flowers can be spoilt by them, though never on a large scale. Eelworms, on the other hand, are a bane, especially when one has just one or two bulbs. They carry a virus that causes the leaves to be deformed, and eventually the whole plant becomes so weak that it dies. There is no cure available to amateur gardeners, so affected bulbs should be thrown away, and fresh bulbs planted away from contaminated soil. Snowdrop bulbs contain lectins, small crystals that are fatal to the intestine, so mice and voles leave them well alone.

PROPAGATION

Propagation is easy, by splitting the clumps regularly after flowering and replanting just before the leaves die back. Do this every other year for the more fragile cultivars like *Galanthus nivalis* 'Sandersii', *elwesii* cultivars and *gracilis*, and every three to four years for more vigorous species and cultivars like *G. plicatus*, 'Atkinsii' and the Greatorex doubles. Many professional gardeners now twin-scale rare snowdrops (peel back two layers attached to a small section of the basal plate), so that each bulb can produce up to 50 new bulbs in three years. This is good news for all potential and confirmed galanthophiles.

Daphnes

With their exquisite fragrance and delicate flowers, daphnes are an excellent choice for the shrub border or alpine garden – and if you are clever, you can have a different daphne flowering all year long. The *Daphne* genus is large, with over 100 species documented, and their shapes and sizes vary enormously. This is influenced in part by their wide geographical distribution, from the freezing inhospitable wilds of the Kamchatka in the far east of Russia down to the sunny islands of the Mediterranean. Although relatively few of these species are in cultivation, there is an ever-increasing number of selected named cultivars and hybrids available in the UK – and it is this tremendous variety that makes it possible to have almost continuous flower and scent throughout the year. I grow more than 50 daphne species and cultivars at my nursery in Somerset and the daphnes I recommend here are ones that perform best in a temperate climate, such as Britain's.

In Greek mythology, Daphne was a nymph and daughter of a river god. Yet despite there being several Greek legends suggesting the origin of the plant name daphne, it is probably not Greek at all, but Indo-European, derived from a word meaning 'odour'. There is evidence that in the past the roots and bark of certain daphnes were used in medicine. They were thought to alleviate cancer, worms, toothache, rheumatism and various skin diseases. Unfortunately, we now know that all parts of daphnes are poisonous. Gastric upsets will result if eaten, while the sap can cause skin irritation.

There are a number of daphnes that make stunning additions to the winter garden with their attractive, scented flowers. Many winter-flowering plants are highly scented, for the simple reason that there are few pollinators around, so they need an extra draw. *Daphne bholua* and its derivatives are generally the largest growing of the cultivated daphnes. Widespread in the Himalayas, they are known as 'paper-

OPPOSITE: *DAPHNE X MAUERBACHII* 'PERFUME OF SPRING', **A GOOD PLANT FOR THE FRONT OF A BORDER. GROWING TO JUST UNDER 1M (40IN), ITS DELICIOUSLY FRAGRANT, CREAMY FLOWERS APPEAR IN LATE SPRING.**

daphnes' since the sinewy bark is used there for paper-making and in the production of rope. They were first introduced to the UK shortly before the Second World War and have an upright habit, growing to 2m (6½ft). They can flower from mid-winter until early spring, depending on the weather. Most are evergreen, but *D. bholua* var. *glacialis* 'Gurkha' is the exception, being totally deciduous. *Daphne bholua* 'Damon Ridge' was originally collected in the wild while *D. b.* 'Jacqueline Postill' (AGM) occurred in cultivation. The flowers of these three are similar, dark pink in bud, opening almost white, with 'Jacqueline Postill' being the pinkest. Distinct in habit and flower is

D.b. 'Alba'. This delightful form tends to have a shorter, bushier habit with pure white flowers.

Another winter-flowering daphne is *D. odora* 'Aureo-marginata', from China and Japan. This is one of the most widely grown daphnes, and the plant that many people first associate with this varied genus. The flowers are typical of daphne, each one being tubular but held in many-flowered clusters on the ends of shoots. They are purple in bud, opening to white with purple staining, which remains on the outside of each flower. It forms a rounded bush of 1.5m (5ft) in all directions. Flowering from late autumn through to late winter, the related *D.* × *hybrida* is a super,

ABOVE LEFT: *D. ALBOWIANA*, **A DISTINCTIVE YELLOW DAPHNE FLOWERING IN EARLY SPRING. ABOVE RIGHT: THE SPRING-FLOWERING** *D. GIRALDII.*
OPPOSITE: *D.* X *BURKWOODII* 'G.K. ARGLES', **A VIGOROUS, VARIEGATED PLANT THAT FLOWERS IN SPRING.**

D. *pontica* (AGM) and D. *albowiana*. These similar species commence flowering in early spring in Britain and have fascinating yellow, almost spidery flowers. First impressions are of little fragrance, but these plants are moth-pollinated so the scent is not released until the evening. Where we live in Somerset, D. *albowiana* flowers a fortnight before D. *pontica* and is slightly smaller growing. Ours are nearly ten years old and have yet to reach 1m (40in) high or wide.

One of the easiest to grow and most rewarding species is D. *tangutica*. First located in Western China in 1873, this evergreen species will make a tidy bush of over 1m (40in) in all directions after ten years. The flowers are very similar to those of D. *odora* – white, tinged purple or pink – and they conveniently follow on as the latter finishes. *Daphne tangutica* will typically start to flower in mid-spring, with full glory in early to midsummer, and will continue sporadically until late autumn; red fruits are subsequently produced. Beware of confusion with its little cousin D. *retusa*. At first glance, this can look identical to D. *tangutica*, but this daphne is much slower growing, eventually making little more than half the size of D. *tangutica*. We also find it less profuse in its flowering, although the individual flowers may be a little larger. It is a good small-scale shrub, possibly best in a rockery, but not quite as reliable and garden-worthy as D. *tangutica*, whose greater vigour makes it more tolerant of adverse conditions.

There are lots of daphnes to enjoy during the summer months. *Daphne × mauerbachii* 'Perfume of Spring' is a winner with its distinctive peachy flowers appearing in late spring. With a tidy habit, it grows to just under 1m (40in) – ideal for the front of a border. Flowering in early to midsummer, D. *altaica* is semi-evergreen with pretty, white star-like flowers. *Daphne × burkwoodii* 'Somerset' is one of a pair of seedlings raised from a deliberate cross made between D. *caucasica* and D. *cneorum* by the Burkwood brothers in 1931. Of good constitution, this sturdy plant is partially evergreen and will reach 1.5m (5ft) tall by 1m (40in) wide.

small-scale evergreen for a sheltered corner. Actually a cross between D. *collina* and D. *odora*, it really does combine the best of both parents, its flowers being the rich, deep pink of D. *collina* but with the scent of D. *odora*. Another popular, widely grown daphne is D. *mezereum* var. *rubra* from central Europe, which grows to about 1.2m (4ft) with a profusion of bright pink flowers clothing the bare branches in early spring. The pure white flowers of the cultivar D. *mezereum* f. *alba* 'Bowles' Variety' create a vivid contrast.

Not quite so dramatic, perhaps, but just as desirable, are

ABOVE: *D. × BURKWOODII* 'LAVENIREI', WHOSE DELICATE, STAR-SHAPED FLOWERS APPEAR IN LATE SPRING.

The flowers are pale pink with a wonderful fragrance, appearing in late spring. The smaller *D. × burkwoodii* 'Lavenirei' has delicate star-shaped flowers. There are also several variegated forms, with scented flowers. The most robust of these is *D. × burkwoodii* 'G. K. Argles', which is upright in habit, its leaves strongly margined with gold. *Daphne × burkwoodii* 'Somerset Gold Edge' is bushier, with cream-edged foliage.

One of my favourite daphnes is *D. × manteniana* 'Manten', a hybrid raised in British Columbia in 1941. A dwarf shrub growing to about 75cm (2½ft), the fragrant, deep rose pink flowers are borne freely from mid-spring over a long period. Another excellent long-flowering hybrid is *D.* 'Richard's Choice'. Named after Richard Lee, who was propagator at Rosemoor until his untimely death in 1993, it was a cross between *D. collina* and *D. × burkwoodii*. The flowers are reminiscent of the latter parent, only larger, and equally well scented. The deciduous *D. giraldii* is also a summer-flowerer, always a talking point with its pretty yellow flowers in mid-summer.

Totally different in habit is *D. cneorum*. Although often considered an alpine due to its prostrate habit, it is too vigorous for most rockeries as it will grow to over 1m (40in) in diameter. The vivid cerise-pink flowers in early summer are very striking but perhaps not the most scented. There are some lovely variants available with white flowers – for example, *D. cneorum* f. *alba*, or *D. cneorum* 'Variegata', which has attractive variegated foliage. Both are eminently suitable for the front of the border. More subtle in its effect is *D. sericea*. This pretty Mediterranean evergreen of tidy upright habit seems to flower sporadically all year with a particular frenzy of colour in early summer. The long narrow leaves have a hairy underside that gives a silvery look to the margins. The deep rose flowers have a delicate, almost translucent appearance.

And so we return to winter. What could be more surprising amid the decay of autumn than to see fresh

leaves appearing as *D. jezoensis* comes to life again; for this amazing plant loses its leaves in spring. The winter flowers are the same tubular shape as the well-known species, but they are an incredible deep, golden yellow and delightfully lemon-scented. Very hard to obtain, but well worth the effort, it forms a rounded bush of 50cm (20in) or less.

Daphnes have a reputation for being difficult to grow, but I urge you to try some of these rewarding plants whose scent can fill the garden with fragrance and colour for so much of the year.

ABOVE: *D. SERICEA,* **A PRETTY MEDITERRANEAN EVERGREEN THAT FLOWERS WITH A PARTICULAR FRENZY OF COLOUR IN EARLY SUMMER.**

ABOVE: **THE PROSTRATE HABIT OF** *D. CNEORUM* 'EXIMIA' **LENDS ITSELF TO A POSITION IN THE FRONT OF THE BORDER.**
OPPOSITE: *D. CNEORUM* 'VARIEGATA'.

PROPAGATION

Daphnes can be difficult to propagate, which is one reason why they are not more readily available. Many species can be grown from seed, but germination can be sporadic. Seed should be sown in containers in a cold frame as soon as it is ripe. Softwood cuttings are another option but, although many daphnes will root quite readily, they can be reluctant to grow away once potted up. The time of year to take cuttings is early to midsummer. Grafting in winter is a more reliable method, assuming that one of the previous steps has been achieved in order to provide a rootstock.

CULTIVATION

The root systems of daphnes have very precise moisture requirements; they hate to be too wet in the winter but do not like to dry out in summer and therefore need a moist but well drained soil in a shady site, protected from the hottest sun. Daphnes object to having hot roots, so mulching with gravel is ideal to reduce evaporation. The daphnes I have mentioned are best grown in a border – on the whole, pots are not a good idea. If they are cut back too hard, they will rarely sprout again. Where essential, trim lightly during the growing season.

PESTS AND DISEASES

Viral infection is responsible for the demise of many a healthy daphne. It is transmitted by aphids, so controlling these will help to prevent healthy plants from being infected. There is no treatment, and such plants are best burnt to minimise the spread of the virus. It shows as a mottling on the foliage, but do not confuse it with yellowing leaves that are naturally about to be shed, or with a plant that is simply hungry. Daphnes do have a reputation for being difficult but their demise is usually a result of weather and site rather than any specific disease of infestation. They do not like extremes of wet or dry.

CURIOSITIES

Sarracenias

Sarracenia is a genus of eight species and several subspecies of deciduous, insect-eating perennials that originate from the southeast of North America. Commonly known as American pitcher plants, they are easy to grow in a cold greenhouse or conservatory, and are becoming more widely available by the minute. Their appeal lies in the fascinating form and colour of their pitchers (leaves) and intriguing flowers – an added bonus in spring. The pitcher plant is one of the easiest and most rewarding carnivorous plants to grow.

Illustrations of *Sarracenia* appear as early as 1576 but it was not until the 18th century that they were named, after the Canadian physician and botanist M. Sarrazine de l'Etang. The first plants were introduced to the UK around 1640 by John Tradescant Junior. In the wild today, most of them are concentrated in the southeastern corner of America, growing in wet, open savanna or swamps. *Sarracenia purpurea* is an exception, spreading north to Canada and round the Great Lakes, where it grows on lake shores and in peat bogs. In the early 1900s it was introduced to peat bogs in Ireland (where it is seen as an invasive weed) and in England, particularly Cumbria. Because of the gradual destruction of their natural habitat, and over-collection both as cut flowers and plants, all species are under threat in the wild, hence their conservation is of great concern.

Sarracenia leaves have developed into pitchers that trap insects, providing nutrients for the plants. Insects such as flies, bees and wasps are attracted to the leaf by its colour, markings and the secretion of nectar around the lip. As the insect investigates the lip of the tube it is lured further down, losing its footing and falling to the bottom of the pitcher. This area has downward-pointing hairs, so the insect is unable to escape, eventually drowning in the digestive juices produced by the plant. All but the hard chitinous parts of the insect are absorbed by the plant as a supplement to its diet.

PREVIOUS PAGE: *ARISAEMA THUNBERGII.*
OPPOSITE: *SARRACENIA* 'OLIVER', **A HYBRID RAISED BY JOHN AND JEAN AINSWORTH.**

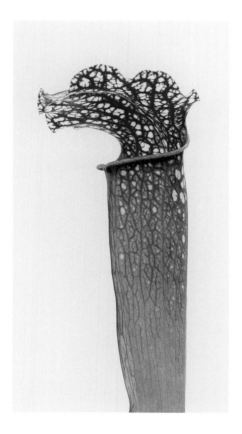 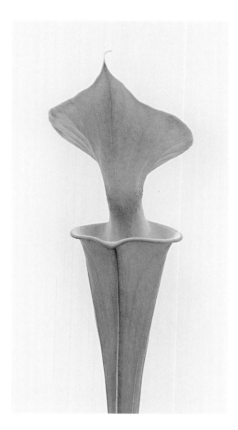 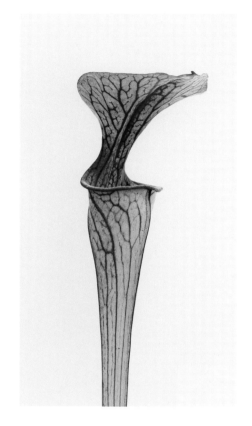

In the wild, sarracenias disperse their seed in autumn. This starts to germinate as the weather warms in late winter or early spring. By the end of the first year's growth, the plants should have developed tiny pitcher leaves a few centimetres long, but they will not reach full maturity for at least five years. Mature plants flower annually, with scented single blooms between late spring and mid-summer, for a period of only a few weeks, and flowers can vary in colour from almost white through yellow to deep ruby-red. The flowers have five large petals that droop around a large umbrella-shaped style. This is retained when the petals drop, forming an attractive seedhead that turns brown as it ripens in autumn. Pollination takes place before the new, young pitchers open in spring, thereby preventing undesirable capture of pollinating insects.

In temperate climates, such as Britain's, sarracenias can be grown either in a greenhouse or outside in full sunlight – the only necessity is that they get enough water. There is an increasing range available to buy and we would suggest the following species and cultivars as being the most rewarding for the average gardener. For both greenhouse and outdoor cultivation, *S. flava* (AGM) or the yellow trumpet is probably the most popular and dramatic of the species, with pitchers reaching 90cm (3ft) in height with a mouth 7 x 5cm (3 x 2in). Pitcher colours range from deep red to palest yellow with a variety of red veining and

ABOVE LEFT: *S. X EXCELLENS.* **ABOVE CENTRE: AN ALL-GREEN FORM OF** *S. FLAVA.* **ABOVE RIGHT:** *S. OREOPHILA.*
OPPOSITE: *S. LEUCOPHYLLA,* **THE WHITE TRUMPET, GOOD FOR GREENHOUSE CULTIVATION AND VERY POPULAR WITH FLORAL ARTISTS.**

a hood that resembles a monk's cowl forming a canopy over the pitcher. The back of the pitcher is covered with 'windows', translucent panels that some writers suggest contribute to the trapping of insects.

Moving out of doors, one of the most popular and hardy sarracenias for the bog garden is *S. purpurea* (the huntsman's cup), because of its short, spreading growth. Protect it from strong winds; the same goes for *S. flava. Sarracenia purpurea* subsp. *venosa* is quite distinctive, but not as hardy, turning bright red to purple when grown in full sun.

Some sarracenia hybrids are equally rewarding to grow. *Sarracenia × catesbyi* is a popular and easily grown hybrid between *S. purpurea* and *S. flava*, which grows well outdoors and colours in full sun to bright yellow with red flushing. Its wide mouth catches large insects. *Sarracenia × wrigleyana* is a cross between *S. psittacina* and *S. leucophylla*, and has the white veining of *S. leucophylla* and delicate red veining. It may be grown outside. *Sarracenia × moorei* was the first man-made cross, between *S. flava* and *S. leucophylla*, made at the National Botanic Gardens at Glasnevin, in Ireland, in 1886. It is perhaps the tallest sarracenia, reaching a height of 1m (40in) under glass – too tall to be grown outdoors for fear of wind damage. One of our own hybrids is *S.* 'Oliver', named after our grandson. A *S. minor* cross, 'Oliver' has the typical 'windows' of that species, but with increased vigour and copper veining late in the season.

While these plants are recommended for easy cultivation and attractiveness, there are others that are less grown, perhaps less garden-worthy, but nonetheless botanically interesting. *Sarracenia psittacina*, for example, is the shortest sarracenia, with curious parrot-beak-shaped pitchers that lie on the ground, attracting creeping insects more than the others. Another small-scale pitcher is *S. rubra*, known as the sweet pitcher plant because of its small, ruby-red sweetly scented flowers. This species and its forms are more of botanical interest, some having straggly early growth.

copper-coloured lids, and its yellow flowers appear in spring. *Sarracenia flava* 'Burgundy' is perhaps one of the better known cultivars, with a 70cm (28in) tall burgundy red pitcher and a heavily veined red lid.

In contrast, *S. leucophylla* (the white trumpet) has beautiful, slender pitchers that can reach 90cm (3ft) in height with the upper part and lid veined in a complex network of green or red on a white background. Look out for a number of variations including *S. leucophylla* 'Schnell's Ghost', a yellow-flowered plant with a very white pitcher top and faint green veining. These are excellent plants for the greenhouse and are becoming very popular with floral artists.

The fascinating *S. minor* (the hooded pitcher plant) has

ABOVE: THE ELEGANT FLOWER OF *S. FLAVA.*

OPPOSITE: *S. × CATESBYI,* **A POPULAR HYBRID THAT GROWS WELL OUTDOORS; ITS WIDE MOUTH CATCHES LARGE INSECTS.**

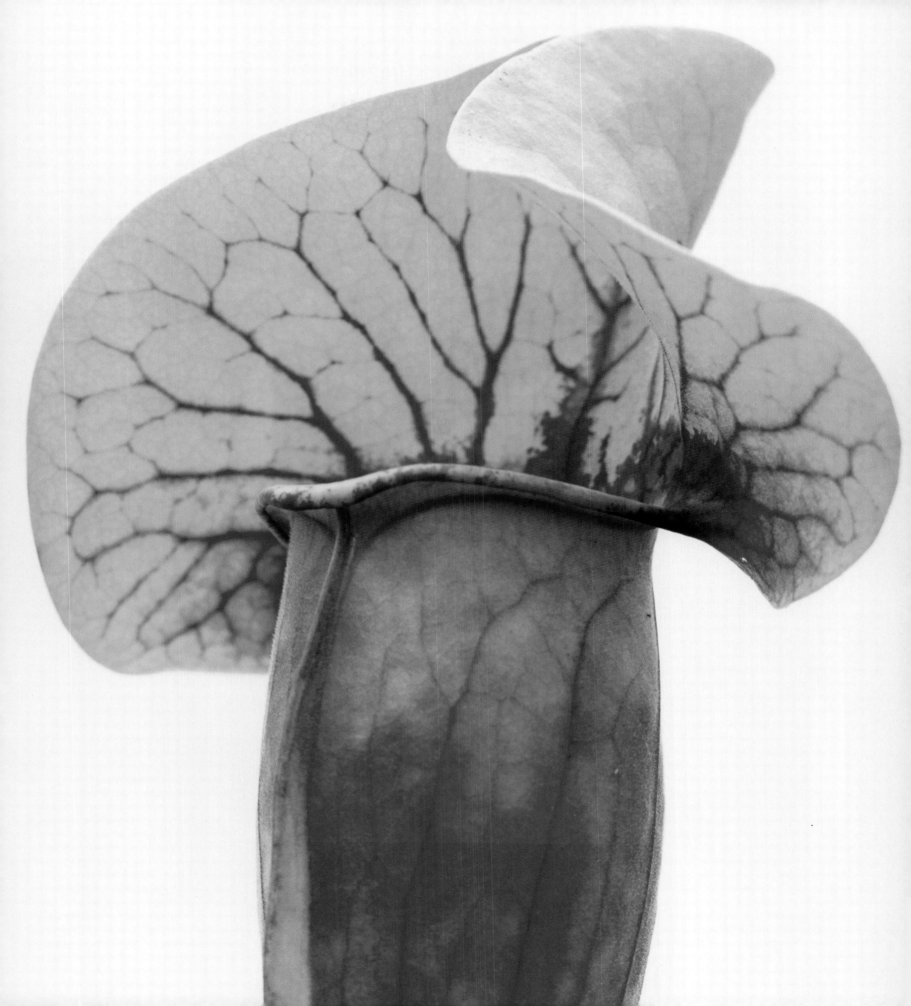

ABOVE: THE CURIOUS PITCHERS OF *S. MINOR,* WHICH RESEMBLE MONKS' COWLS. THE WHITE SPOTS ARE TRANSLUCENT PANELS, WHICH SOME SUGGEST CONTRIBUTE TO THE TRAPPING OF PREY.

CULTIVATION

In America, sarracenia's natural habitats are typically wet, nutrient-deficient sphagnum bogs, so when cultivating them, these conditions must be recreated as far as possible. Of course most people do not have a large open piece of land in which to plant them, but this is not critical – as long as they are kept moist all year round, sarracenias will do well in temperate climates in a cold greenhouse or outside in a bog garden in milder areas, preferably in full sun. During the growing season, they should stand in up to 5cm (2in) of water when grown under cover; preferably this should be rainwater as hard water or chlorinated mains water is detrimental to growth. In winter, a cool, moist period of at least six weeks to grow slowly is beneficial and the plants will withstand freezing to about -15°C (5°F). When planting in pots, use a compost made up from four parts good-quality sphagnum peat, one part coarse, lime-free sand and one part Perlite. We use 5cm (2in) pots for the youngest seedlings and grade them upwards as the plants get bigger. It is best to keep them in a tray that will retain water, but never feed them as they receive the nutrients they need from the insects they catch. Outside, sarracenias should ideally be in full sun and protected from the wind. The soil should be peaty and permanently wet.

PESTS AND DISEASES

Common pests are greenfly in the early season and scale insects later on, both of which can be controlled using systemic insecticide at half strength. In winter, botrytis (grey mould) may develop as the pitcher dies down. Control it using fungicide, (not copper-based), and maintain good air circulation. As the pitchers die back the dead parts should be removed.

PROPAGATION

The easiest way to propagate sarracenias is by division, as mature plants produce offshoots and new growing points every year. Plants start into growth in early spring and flower before the pitchers open so, for established plants, you should re-pot before growth starts. Divide by cutting the rhizome between the growing centres, carefully potting each piece. Use dry compost rather than moist, so it fills in around the roots, and then soak thoroughly. Short pieces of rhizome may be removed to make more plants from dormant buds.

Propagating by seed is an alternative, and the seed is easily germinated if it is fresh – but you will have to be patient, as it will take five years to produce a flowering plant. Seed is ripe in mid-autumn when the pod splits, and it may be sown immediately or kept dry in a sealed container over winter in a fridge. The seed will benefit from a cool, moist treatment, mixing it with a small quantity of finely chopped sphagnum moss or moist peat kept at about 2°C (35°F) for six weeks before sowing. Sow the seeds on the surface of 5cm (2in) pots filled with sphagnum peat (the seeds should not be covered) and stand in about 2.5cm (1in) of rain water. Germination, at a temperature of 16°C (60°F), will take about four weeks, after which the seedlings should stand in light airy conditions on a windowsill or greenhouse bench – make sure they do not dry out. Leave them in a pot for the first year and then prick out into seed trays or individual 5cm (2in) pots. Seed may be sown at any time from early spring to autumn.

Pitcher plants are fascinating, and relatively easy to grow. If you are tempted to try them, we would advise you start with low-priced unnamed mature seedlings to gain experience. Subsequently, some of the easier-to-grow species – perhaps *Sarracenia flava* or *S. purpurea* – as well as some of the more vigorous hybrids – such as *S.* × *catesbyi* or *S.* × *moorei* – are all most attractive and rewarding.

Proteas

By late winter, some gardeners in temperate climates may have tired of holly and ivy, but the glorious colours of proteas, which bloom all through winter and into spring, provide an exotic alternative. The genus, native to the African continent, consists of some 100 species, and is a member of the *Proteaceae* family. I have visited the Cape Floral Kingdom in South Africa to study proteas in their natural habitat and currently there are nearly 20 species growing in the temperate climate of the Isle of Tresco, where I live and work.

Protea… 'the handsomest of plants, whether for size, form or colour of inflorescence; would carry away the first prize at any horticultural show.' Sir Joseph Hooker's observations on the protea, from *Curtis's Botanical Magazine*, are as fitting now as they were in 1881. The allure of the protea's bract-encased flower has not diminished, nor has its variety. The namesake of both genus and family is Proteus, a deity from Greek mythology, whose talents included the ability to change shape at will. It is an example of gifted nomenclature. The protea can amaze, however, for reasons other than comeliness and mutability. The delights of the proteas of the Western Cape seem at odds with their environment – it is extraordinary that such extravagance should issue from such an unforgiving land.

The majority of protea species are to be found in the Fynbos, the heath and shrub land that dominates the Cape Floral Kingdom. The Fynbos is characterised by a flora of immense diversity, but it is an area low in soil nutrients and beleaguered by summer drought; raging fires are part of the natural cycle and the protea family has learnt to survive these adverse conditions. The earliest fossil evidence of *Proteaceae* goes back some 95 million years, so the protea has had time to adapt itself well.

In order to produce such lavish blooms, proteas must squeeze as much value as possible from the environment. The glories above ground are matched by incredible

OPPOSITE: **THE BRIGHT PINK HAIRY BRACTS OF** *PROTEA COMPACTA* **MAKE A SPLASH IN SPRING AND SUMMER.**

ingenuity beneath. Proteas are evergreen and, as profligacy means death in the Fynbos, nothing is wasted. As the winter rains approach, the oldest leaves translocate nutrients to the newer foliage, after which they fall. The leaf litter begins to rot and, in the period between wet and dry seasons, the protea must harvest what little nutrient is available. This it does by augmenting its permanent root system with its *piéce de résistance* – proteoid roots. These are clusters of rootlets formed along the existing root structure, just below the surface of the soil. They resemble fragments of cotton wool and may more than double the mass of the usual system. They are twice as efficient at picking up water and nutrients as normal roots. The reward for such industry is the magnificent flowerhead of the protea.

But there is a downside. The proteoid roots, like many precision instruments, are extremely sensitive. Adept at absorbing precious nourishment, they seem to lack any mechanism to regulate consumption, and can sometimes absorb too many nutrients, particularly phosphates, which leads to the extinction of the plant. This susceptibility has

ABOVE: A DWARF FORM OF THE SPECTACULAR *P. CYNAROIDES,* OR KING PROTEA.
OPPOSITE: *P. LANCEOLATA,* ONE OF THE EASIEST PROTEAS TO GROW IN A TEMPERATE CLIMATE.

helped the protea acquire a reputation for being temperamental in cultivation. This is not wholly justified, because the protea has been successfully grown even in Britain and parts of Europe.

Proteas were first cultivated in Britain in the 18th century and were, at this time, seen as the height of horticultural fashion. Before the establishment of Kirstenbosch Botanic Gardens in South Africa, the greatest collection in cultivation had been held in London, with a total of 35 species recorded in 1805. It belonged to George Hibbert, an MP and wealthy merchant. Members of the

aristocracy vied for seed, and enthusiasts included George III and the Empress Josephine. Hibbert's collection was kept in large pots and housed in Clapham. The plants were overwintered under glass, but wheeled outside in the spring, after the last of the frosts.

The bloom of a protea is made up of many individual flowers, contained in a receptacle of ornamental bracts. A single species may have many colour variations within it, with separate plants producing bracts from green to carmine. These bracts may be tipped with hairs, known as beards. This bearding can also be evident on the individual flowers themselves, giving the appearance of a furry cone, called an awn, within the flowerhead. The flowerheads are not the only source of ornament. The leaves of *Protea eximia*, for example, can take on a most attractive purple hue, while many young leaves are covered in soft hairs.

One of the earliest species of protea to have been brought to flower in Europe was *P. lepidocarpodendron*, whose creamy bracts are tipped with purple-black bearding. It can grow 2–3m (6½–10ft) tall, flowering from late autumn through to the spring, when flowers are profuse. *Protea neriifolia* is similar in stature and has the same long flowering period, but its bracts vary from cream to carmine. Both species have endured 100-mile-per-hour, salt-laden gales on Tresco, with apparent nonchalence. *Protea neriifolia* can be found at altitudes of up to 1,300m (4,265ft) in the Western Cape, and can tolerate light frost of about -3C (26°F). Another bearded protea, *P. magnifica*, is one of the most frost-hardy of species, growing in rock cracks up to 2,700m (8,858ft) high, well into the winter snowline. The splendid array of *P. magnifica*, or the queen protea, coupled with its hardiness, has made the plant a favourite for hybridisation. These hybrids are not necessarily more handsome than the species, but the result is an enhanced commercial viability for the cut-flower market.

A protea that has hybridised naturally with *P. magnifica* is *P. longifolia*, one of the most promiscuous of the genus.

ABOVE: THE INTRICATE BUD OF *P. LONGIFOLIA.*

Protea longifolia is a sprawling shrub, remarkable for its large black and woolly awn. *Protea burchellii*, equally, does not become a shrub of grand proportions, growing to a maximum of 2m (6½ft). As with many proteas, the bract colour varies enormously from cream to pink. It is an adaptable plant, flowering solidly from late winter to early summer on Tresco, and copes well with hot, dry positions.

Proteas can grow quite large, and *P. mundii* is one of the tallest. A specimen was found that was over 11m (36ft) high in the Western Cape, though the norm is between 3–8m (10–26ft). It is blessed with a long flowering period that begins in mid-winter, on Tresco, with flowers still opening in late summer. Like many proteas, it is a fast grower. It will take some frost and can adapt to a variety of soil types, but prefers well drained and slightly acid conditions.

In general, proteas favour acidic soils, but there are exceptions. The easily grown and delicately flowered *P. lanceolata* can be found on calcareous white sand in the wild. *Protea susannae* is also found naturally on neutral or calcareous sandy soil. This species is viewed with some circumspection by flower arrangers, as its leaves, if crushed, exude an unwholesome odour of bad eggs. Afrikaaners refer to it as *stinkblaarsuikerbos*: translation is superfluous. The smell is, at least, a welcome aid to the bemused botanist.

The most easily recognised of all proteas must be the king protea, *P. cynaroides*, the national flower of South Africa. For adaptability and ease of cultivation it is one of the best of all. By way of protection against fire, the king protea has a lignotuber – a woody base that serves as a store of energy and buds. The large flowerheads last well and come in a variety of forms, including a dwarf variant, ideal for the smaller garden. The flowerheads of *P. aurea* subsp. *potbergensis* (endemic to Potberg in the Cape) are not so long lived. They do show, however, that a protea's ornamental worth is not confined to full flower. The buds sit upright like candles and, even when all colour has faded, the shuttlecock form of the flower when over is

most arresting. *Protea compacta* is similar to *P. aurea* in its undisciplined growth habit, but its pink blooms make up for the lack of order.

Proteas, then, provide an exotic challenge for the gardener – but not as formidable a one as perceived. The most important elements in their cultivation are an acidic or neutral, well drained soil, a sunny position, good ventilation, not too many nutrients, and protection from severe frost. It is hoped that the examples here form a brief and general introduction to its diverse and ornamental forms, while also celebrating one of the floral alchemists of the Fynbos.

ABOVE: A *P. LONGIFOLIA* **HYBRID.**

ABOVE: *P. SUSANNAE,* **A PLANT BLESSED WITH A SIX-MONTH FLOWERING SEASON.**
OPPOSITE LEFT: *P. LEPIDOCARPODENDRON.* **OPPOSITE RIGHT:** *P. NERIIFOLIA.*

CULTIVATION

Despite being a tender genus in the main, many of the montane species of protea will take a few degrees of frost, although young plants should always be given frost protection. Good drainage is essential, whether grown in a pot or in the ground – never allow the roots to become soggy. Proteas are averse to still and warm humidity, preferring to feel the wind in their leaves. For this reason, if plants are given indoor protection during heavy frosts, they should be well ventilated. If growing in a relatively mild climate, plants can be left outside, but cover with fleece in heavy frosts. Where temperatures regularly fall below freezing, I recommend keeping the plants in pots to be brought inside in the winter.

PROPAGATION

To grow from seed, soak seed in warm water (50–60°C/ 122–140°F) for 15–30 minutes and then leave to dry on newspaper prior to sowing. Seed will germinate most successfully when on or near the surface of the medium. For best results, seed should be as fresh as possible. I recommend purchasing seed from Silverhill Seeds in Cape Town, who will send good quality seed all over the world. If removing seeds from old flowerheads, it is sometimes necessary to warm the heads gently to encourage them to release the seeds. Leave overnight in a warm place (30°C/86°F). Semi-hard cuttings of 15–20cm (6–8in) length can be taken in autumn. Potting mixes should be acidic, low in nutrients and very well drained.

Passion flowers

The climbing tendrils and exotic blooms of the passion flower may be synonymous with the steamy tropics, but there are some species that can be grown outdoors in the temperate British climate, and lots more that will thrive in a heated conservatory or greenhouse.

The earliest record of a plant that we would now consider a passion flower is that of Pedro de Cieza in 1553. The earliest known illustration dates back to 1609 and is a drawing of the flower as a religious symbol of Christ's passion or crucifixion. The name passion flower, however, did not appear in literature for another 50 years. In 1610 a monastic scholar, Jacomo Bosio, learnt of this wondrous flower, and is credited with popularising the religious importance of the plant. Jesuit priests travelling to the New World saw natives eating the fruit of these holy vines, and took it as a sign that they were hungry for Christianity. Today, the legend is still associated with the passion flower, particularly with *Passiflora caerulea*, the blue passion flower, since this is the most commonly cultivated species in Europe. Every part of the flower has symbolic significance, for example the three stigmas represent the three nails that held Christ on the cross, the five stamens are the five wounds, and the corona filaments represent the crown of thorns.

Native to a wide range of natural habitats from the high Andean mountains to the tropics of Asia, the *Passiflora* genus embraces 521 species of mostly evergreen plants. Most passion flowers are vigorous climbing vines and some, like *P. quadrangularis* (the giant granadilla), may grow to 50m (164ft) in South America and the West Indies. Most species aren't quite as robust as this but are, nevertheless, quite prolific if given the chance. *Passiflora tarminiana* (known so well as *P. mollissima*), the banana passion flower, will clamber over anything in its path, even mountains, and is so rampant that it is now classified as a pernicious weed in Hawaii and parts of New Zealand, where it was introduced for its sweet, aromatic, banana-shaped fruit in the

OPPOSITE: *PASSIFLORA CAERULEA* **IS THE MOST COMMON PASSION FLOWER IN EUROPE, AND WILL FLOURISH IN TEMPERATE CLIMATES.**

North America deep underground, where the thick, fleshy roots remain comparatively dry and protected beneath the frozen surface and thick snow. Unfortunately, the wet winter soil conditions of the UK are not ideal for this species, but a sheltered spot beneath the eaves of a house should give sufficient protection for it to overwinter successfully. There are even a couple of true tree passion flowers. *Passiflora lindeniana* is very rarely seen, with only two known mature specimens left (in Venezuela), and *P. foetida* (stink weed) is found wild in most of the tropics and sub-tropics of the Americas, and also now in many parts of Asia and Australia. Its fruits are quite small and usually bright red, orange or yellow and are a great favourite with children. Recently it has been discovered that this plant is actually carnivorous – the numerous sticky, nectar-bearing glands on the feathery bracts that surround the flowerbuds attract and trap insects. The plants then supplement their nutritional intake by absorbing nitrates from their prey.

Passion flowers exist in a wide range of natural habitats in the wild, from high mountains to semi-desert. But, apart from a few lowland tropical species that are found on the flood plains or wet forests of South America, passion flowers are always found growing on very well drained soil. This is of great importance when cultivating plants in pots, or when they are planted outside in temperate regions, where they might be standing in cold soil for several months each year. The traditional position for growing a passion flower is against a south- or west-facing house wall and this works well for most species. Passion flowers are mostly evergreens and bloom on new growth during spring and summer. The flowering period is dependent on the individual position and microclimate surrounding each vine. Recently, with very mild autumns and winters, *P. caerulea* has still been flowering in early winter here in the southwest of England.

19th century. Over 40 species are cultivated for their edible fruit in South and Central America, most of which are simply picked and eaten when ripe or made into refreshing cold drinks. There are a few species, such as *P. edulis* and *P. tarminiana*, that are of economic importance and many thousands of tonnes of fruit are harvested each year in countries such as Australia, New Zealand, South Africa and the Americas, to be processed into drinks, sherbets, sweets and, more recently, shower gels, soaps and even joss-sticks.

Passiflora incarnata is unusual in that it is truly herbaceous and survives the severe winter conditions of

Of the myriad species in existence, relatively few can be cultivated in the cooler climates of Europe, but nevertheless

ABOVE: *P. X KEWENSIS,* **SUITABLE FOR GROWING OUTSIDE IN A SHELTERED SPOT.**

OPPOSITE: **THE FRAGRANT WHITE FLOWERS OF** *P. CAERULEA* 'CONSTANCE ELLIOT'.

there are enough to make a small collection worthwhile. *Passiflora caerulea* and its cultivar *P. c.* 'Constance Elliott' are undoubtedly the best tried and tested passion flowers for the outdoor garden. *Passiflora caerulea*, the blue passion flower, is probably the one that most people will associate with the genus, and it flourishes all over the UK, including cooler parts of Scotland and North Wales. Both are vigorous and free-flowering and can cover the side of a house in five years. However, unlike ivies and Virginia creepers, they do not have adventurous roots that can damage a house's walls. Instead they climb using tendrils and must be supported on wires or trellis. Large blue and white flowers (*P. caerulea*) or pure white flowers

(*P. c.* 'Constance Elliott') are produced throughout summer and autumn, and are followed by attractive, bright orange fruit that may remain on the vine until late winter. Although not usually harvested, these fruit are edible and the taste, although a little insipid, is rather pleasant with a mild blackberry flavour.

There are many other passion flowers worth considering, particularly for the sheltered city garden or unheated conservatory. *Passiflora tarminiana*, *P. mixta* and *P. manicata* are all from the high Andean mountains where they tolerate the occasional slight frost, and are available from a few nurseries in the UK. Both *P. tarminiana* and *P. mixta* produce a profusion of large, soft pink, pendular flowers

ABOVE LEFT: THE VIBRANT JELLY-FISH-LIKE TENDRILS OF *P.* 'INCENSE'. ABOVE RIGHT: LEMON-YELLOW *P. CITRINA* IS A SMALL-FLOWERED SPECIES.

with very long calyx tubes. In the wild the flowers are pollinated by long-billed hummingbirds. In contrast, the smaller, brilliant-red flowers of *P. manicata* are held vertically and are pollinated by large bees.

Passiflora trisecta is also found in high mountains in Peru and is strictly a night-flowering species, pollinated by bats that are rewarded for their services with abundant quantities of sweet nectar. This must be the choice of the workaholic who works all available daylight hours and can then come home and enjoy his passiflora at midnight. *Passiflora trisecta* is available from my own nursery, but not from many others in the UK – a pity because it is spectacular when seen by moonlight. *Passiflora edulis* has delightfully fragrant flowers and produces large edible fruit. *Passiflora actinia* is a great favourite in the US because of the abundant attractive blue-and-white fragrant flowers it produces in early spring. It is beautifully scented and will tolerate slight frosts. *Passiflora × decaisneana* and *P.* 'Byron Beauty' may survive in very sheltered gardens, although it may be worth rooting a few cuttings and keeping them indoors for the winter as a precaution. Very recently, a few more cultivars have been released: *P.* 'Andy' and *P.* 'Simply Red' are doing very well in garden trials, but *P.* 'Pura Vida' and *P.* 'Sapphire' seem better suited to a frost-free greenhouse or conservatory. With all tender passion flowers it is always worth taking a few cuttings to overwinter indoors in case of a severe winter. *Passiflora × kewensis* is an old favourite that might do well in a very sheltered spot but it is perhaps better suited to the frost-protected conservatory.

Gardeners with a heated conservatory that is kept at a minimum temperature of 10–15°C (50–59°F) can grow a wide range of spectacular species and cultivars. These range from old favourites like *P. × decaisneana*, with its huge, heavy, 12cm (5in) diameter blooms of deep red, purple and white, to *P. vitifolia*, a rainforest species with crimson flowers and its hybrid *P. × piresae* with pure red flowers up

to 15cm (6in) wide. Both will overwinter at these temperatures and, apart from a short period in early spring, will flower all year round. There are numerous named varieties of *P. foetida* that will grow to 2.5m (8ft), with an endless succession of flowers and fruit in their first season. For fragrance, another favourite, particularly in the US, is *P. helleri*, which has small, purple-white flowers and deep green foliage. Many small-flowered species – such as *P. capsularis*, with its vanilla-white flowers, *P. citrina*, with citrus-yellow flowers and *P.* 'Adularia', which sports peach-coloured flowers – are very easy to grow in the conservatory. The unusual and wonderful *P. penduliflora* features pale green and orange flowers that hang on long, fragile peduncles.

ABOVE: *P. X DECAISNEANA,* A PASSION FLOWER FOR THE CONSERVATORY. INDOOR PASSION FLOWERS SHOULD BE KEPT AT NO LESS THAN 10°C (50°F) AND, MOST IMPORTANTLY, SHOULD BE PLANTED IN FREE-DRAINING COMPOST.

ABOVE: *P. COCCINEA,* THE RED GRANADILLA, ORIGINATES FROM BOLIVIA AND IS A GREAT FAVOURITE FOR HEATED CONSERVATORIES.
OPPOSITE: *P. EDULIS* 'NORFOLK'. ITS DISTINCTIVE WHITE FLOWERS HAVE WAVY CORONAS AND DEVELOP INTO EDIBLE PURPLE FRUITS IN AUTUMN.

CULTIVATION

The most important condition for growing passion flowers is a well drained soil (particularly if growing in pots or outside where they may be standing in cold soil for several months). A south- or west-facing wall is often the best bet, but the orientation is not as important as the overall light intensity. Good light is essential, but they can be damaged if scorched. Many species, especially those from high mountains, such as *Passiflora tarminiana*, *P. manicata* and *P. mixta*, do well outdoors and overwinter well, providing they do not have to tolerate prolonged sub-zero temperatures and sodden soil. An occasional slight frost of -2°C (28°F) for one or two hours will do little harm. However, some protection is advisable if frosts are prolonged. If you are overwintering them in pots outdoors, roots will suffer permanent damage if the pot is allowed to freeze. Thermal protection around the base of the vine is advisable, and keeping the pots close to a house wall is a must. Raising the pots off the ground will also help. The plants may be pruned, but this should be done with care, and not until new growth is established in late spring. Throughout the summer you can prune lightly, but only cut out dead and unwanted shoots. Try to resist the temptation to have a tidy-up in the autumn or winter with a hard pruning of the vines as this will do them no good.

Passion flowers are eminently deserving of a place in the conservatory but the most important point to remember is not to over-pot young plants. Re-pot when necessary, into a slightly larger pot each time, but not in autumn or winter when plants are growing slowly. As for watering, if in doubt, don't. The ancient ancestors of passion flowers were desert-dwelling plants and the ability of today's plants to tolerate dry conditions seems to have been inherited from these forbears. Finally, always use a well drained compost. I prefer a soil-based kind, but humus-rich compost with extra grit produces good results.

PROPAGATION

Most species and cultivars are easily propagated by taking cuttings during the spring or summer. They should always be taken from healthy, vigorously growing shoots and should be prepared as nodal cuttings. Take cuttings with three nodes and trim the stem 5mm (¼in) above the top node. Trim directly underneath the base node and carefully remove the leaf stalk, tendrils and stipules with a knife or scissors. Secateurs are best avoided as they tend to cause extensive bruising that is an invitation to bacteria or fungus. Cuttings should be dipped in hormone rooting powder and inserted into small pots of sand or peat. Put them on a windowsill with a plastic bag over the top or, better still, in a propagator at 21–26°C (69–78°F). Spring and summer cuttings should root within three to four weeks. Or propagate from seed – why not? Most seed will germinate within four weeks if sown in seed compost and kept at 21–26°C (69–78°F), although some, particularly that of some of the rarer species, is very reluctant to germinate. It may also be worth remembering that plants grown from seed may not come true, whereas plants from cuttings will be exact replicas.

Arisaemas

Arisaemas are intriguing garden plants. Their bizarre, almost animal-like appearance is reflected in common names such as cobra plant and dragon root. Until about a decade ago, only the most devoted fanciers grew them and they were virtually impossible to obtain. Now, however, they are easier to find, with about 60 species listed in the *RHS Plant Finder*.

The first arisaema to be grown in England was *Arisaema triphyllum*, or Jack-in-the-pulpit, from eastern North America, which was introduced around 1664. Until the late 1880s, however, few others were cultivated, but species such as *A. griffithii* and *A. nepenthoides* from the Himalayas were soon joined by Chinese species. A trickle of new species resulted from the great plant-hunting expeditions of the early 1900s. *Arisaema candidissimum*, for example, was discovered in western China by George Forrest in 1914. But most of the plants grown today have been introduced (or reintroduced) since the 1970s.

Modern-day plant hunters such as Bleddyn and Sue Wynn-Jones of Crûg Farm in Wales are bringing back many exciting new species from abroad, and offer an extensive choice in their current list.

The genus as a whole consists of about 170 species native to eastern North America, the Himalayas, some parts of Asia and ranging westwards into East Africa. Related to *Arum* (sometimes known as lords and ladies), arisaemas are curious-looking plants, not always pretty, but strangely attractive. Some look like mice, others resemble elephants, snakes or dragons, others are just weird and fantastic. Their complex 'flowers' comprise the spathe (sheath) and spadix (fleshy spike), at the base of which are minute, separate male and female flowers. Their foliage is usually most elegant, providing shapes, textures and forms not displayed by other plants. Some are like beautiful parasols or miniature palm trees. Others are huge trefoils, and yet others look like fleshy horse-chestnut leaves. They

OPPOSITE: *ARISAEMA ELEPHAS* ORIGINATES FROM CHINA, AND ALTHOUGH RARELY SEEN IN EUROPE, IT IS REASONABLY HARDY.

fellow. The spadix is short, green and striped, covered by the hooded spathe that is pale green striped with purple inside. Native Americans cooked and ate its tubers, so it is also known as Indian turnip.

Arisaema candidissimum is one of the species discovered in western China in 1914 by George Forrest. It was introduced into Britain some years later, and received an AGM from the Royal Horticultural Society when shown by Arthur Bulley of Ness Botanic Gardens, in Liverpool, in 1924. Thoroughly deserving of a place in every garden, it is exquisitely beautiful, with candy-striped white and pink spathes, followed by large, pale green, three-lobed leaves. Naturalised in a woodland garden, *A. candidissimum* is a splendid sight when it blooms in midsummer, looking like a mass of white and pink paper lanterns.

In the past decade, a host of previously unfamiliar species have come into cultivation, and some arisaemas that were grown in only a few gardens during the 1930s have been reintroduced and made more readily available. Of the latter, I give pride of place to *A. sikokianum*, which comes from Japan. In 1997 I was delighted to see this plant in almost every garden in north western America, not as solitary specimens but as flourishing clumps. The dramatic, pure white spadix has an expanded knob at the end, and looks just like the porcelain pestles used to grind spices. This is enclosed within a dark purple, striped spathe. The pair of leaves, one five-lobed, the other three-lobed, emerges in early spring, which means that I have problems growing it in my Norfolk garden. Late spring frosts destroy the newly emerged foliage. This species needs to be planted in a well sheltered place – under trees in the dappled shade of a woodland garden is ideal – or kept in an unheated but frost proof glasshouse. One way of trying to delay its emergence until the frosts have ceased is to plant the tubers deeply, say to 25–35cm (10–14in) deep. Indeed, this also applies to other early arisaemas.

range from pale sea-green to rich, glossy dark green. Reginald Farrer, in *The English Rock Garden* (1976), characterised *Arisaema* as having handsome foliage with 'dingy great Arum-flowers, often hooded over and ending in a long rat-tail wisp'.

Before the 1980s, when inquisitive plant collectors visiting eastern Asia began to gather seeds and introduce other species, almost the only arisaema commonly seem in gardens were *A. triplyllum* or *A. candidissimum* from western China. While *A. triphyllum* is not spectacular, I agree with Graham Stuart Thomas that it is an elegant, amusing

ABOVE: *A. CANDIDISSIMUM,* **PROBABLY THE MOST WIDELY-GROWN ARISAEMA.**

OPPOSITE: *A. SPECIOSUM,* **A HANDSOME PLANT FROM THE EASTERN HIMALAYAS AND CHINA, BEST GROWN UNDER GLASS.**

There are many other arisaemas to try if you are intrigued. An easy one, for starters, is the usually yellow *A. flavum*, which occurs throughout Asia from Yemen to China, and grows happily in the open. It has a small spathe – one of the shortest in the genus – that ranges in colour from green to bright yellow, and resembles a baby canary sitting on a top of a stem. I have found this quite a hardy species; it grew well outdoors in Dublin. Another species that survived for many years in an open, sunny spot in Dublin is *A. erubescens*. This has a single leaf, like a little palm tree, with ten or more elliptical leaflets radiating from the stalk and forming an umbrella over the elegant green spathe.

Another Himalayan species is *A. speciosum*, an extraordinary plant and very striking, but less hardy, so probably best grown in a glasshouse. It has a long, rat-tail spadix with a velvety, dark purple spathe striped with white. This arches forward over the spadix, which has a very long, dangling tail at least 45cm (1½ft) long. The three-lobed leaf is held aloft on a purple stalk, and the leaflets are a rich, dark green with prominent veins.

One of my favourites is *A. griffithii* from the Himalayas. I have only just acquired this, so I cannot relate how well

ABOVE LEFT: THE THREAD-LIKE *A. TAIWANENSE* HAS MOTTLED STEMS THAT CAN REACH UP TO 1.5M (5FT) TALL.

ABOVE RIGHT: THE DRAMATIC SPADIX OF *A. SIKOKIANUM,* WHICH COMES FROM JAPAN.

it does in Norfolk, but I have seen it flourishing in Ireland. Each tuber produces two broad, three-lobed leaves. Then comes the spathe, likened sometimes to a cobra's hood – purple, green and whitish-grey. The spadix is enveloped by the spathe, except for the threadlike tip, which may dangle to the ground.

Sue and Bleddyn Wynn-Jones are among the most experienced arisaema collectors and growers in Britain. At their nursery at Crûg Farm in Wales they grow about 40 different species, and they assure me that in years to come even more will be available, including Chinese species with sweetly fragrant flowers. When asked what his favourite was, Bleddyn immediately picked out *A. taiwanense*, which can grow to 1.5m (5ft) tall. Its stems are beautifully mottled with purplish brown. The solitary, palm-like leaf has up to 15 leaflets, each with very long tips. The spathe is purple and also has a threadlike tip. Bleddyn also admires *A. kiushianum* from Japan, which has an owl-eyed spathe that lurks under the foliage. Crûg's list also included *A. dracontium*, known as the dragon plant in its native east North America; the Himalayan *A. jacquemontii*, an elegant plant with a narrow, light green, white-striped spathe; and *A. thunbergii* subsp. *urashima* from Japan, a moderately hardy plant growing to about 50cm (20in).

If I had to pick a favourite, it would be *A. costatum*, which has settled well into my Norfolk garden. It is very handsome, with an enormous solitary leaf. Each of the three, elliptical leaflets is more that 30cm (1ft) long, rich green and glossy with impressed veins. You have to look underneath to see the flower. The spathe is dark purple, almost black with translucent white lines – when it catches a beam of sunlight, it is sumptuous. *Arisaema costatum* is a midsummer riser, and will grow happily even in a plastic pot. In autumn, the leaflets turn butter-yellow before melting away.

In general, arisaemas are woodland plants, flourishing in moist but well drained soil with a good covering of leaf mould on top. They usually need dappled shade but a few will tolerate full sun. Their tubers should remain moist at all times – but don't allow them to become waterlogged. This is prevented by placing a thick cushion of grit under each tuber when planting, and by choosing a site with good drainage. The hardy arisaemas are easy to accommodate outside, whereas the more frost-sensitive ones can be overwintered in a cool glasshouse. Although it is best to grow arisaemas in a woodland garden, or in a shaded, raised bed, they can also be grown in pots. Once planted, try not to disturb the tubers – leave them alone, and if they are happy, they will thrive.

ABOVE: *A. FLAVUM.*

ABOVE: *A. JACQUEMONTII,* FROM THE HIMALAYAS, HAS A DISTINCTIVE, LONG, THREAD-LIKE TAIL RISING ABOVE THE SPATHE.
OPPOSITE: *A. COSTATUM.*

CULTIVATION

If growing outdoors, choose a lightly shaded site where the soil is moist but very well drained. Dig in plenty of leaf mould or well rotted compost. Dig a hole 30cm (12in) deep, put about 10cm (4in) grit under each tuber and cover with soil. In a cool glasshouse, use a free-draining mixture of loam, grit, sand and leaf mould. Plant tubers about 15–20cm (6–8in) deep in clay pots, and place in a brightly lit place, shaded from direct sun. Water regularly when in growth; feed with low-nitrogen liquid fertiliser once a month. Pots can be put outside when frosts have ceased.

PROPAGATION

Arisaema tubers produce offsets. These can be removed when re-potting pot-grown plants, and then potted on. For species planted out in open ground, offsets can be carefully removed in late summer. Water well and note that sometimes offsets remain dormant and do not sprout in their first year. Seed should be sown in autumn or spring in a free-draining mixture of loam, grit, sand and leaf mould. Keep the compost moist but make sure it is not too wet. Seeds of hardy species will germinate readily if left in a cold frame. Sub-tropical species can also be treated in this way. Note that germination may take several months. Leave seedlings undisturbed, or if you have sown them thickly, prick out clusters into pots when large enough to handle. Re-pot the small tubers individually after the foliage has died down in autumn, or wait until they have reached flowering size and then separate.

WHERE TO FIND AND SEE THE PROFILED PLANTS

This list is arranged alphabetically by plant, and features suppliers recommended by *Gardens Illustrated* magazine. You will also find information about relevant collections and societies. All addresses and contact details can be found on pages 226–232.

ARISAEMAS (pages 214–221)

SUPPLIERS
Paul Christian Rare Plants, Wales
Crûg Farm Plants, Wales
Elizabeth Town Nursery, Australia
Plant Delights Nursery, USA
Gary and Sue Reid, Australia
Red's Rhodies, USA
Seneca Hill Perennials, USA
Yamina Rare Plants, Australia

COLLECTIONS AND SOCIETIES
Missouri Botanical Garden, USA

CORYDALIS (pages 38–45)

SUPPLIERS
Avon Bulbs, England
Paul Christian Rare Plants, Wales
Christie's Nursery, Scotland
Digger's Club, Australia
Elizabeth Town Nursery, Australia
Fraser's Thimble Farms, Canada
Russell Graham Purveyor of Plants, USA
Hartside Nursery Garden, England
Hythe Alpines, England
Janis Ruksans Bulb Nursery, Latvia
Merry Garth, Australia
Paradise Centre, England
Potterton & Martin, England
Tesselaar Bulbs & Flowers, Australia
Wychwood Plants, Australia

COLLECTIONS AND SOCIETIES
The Botanic Garden, Sweden
Heronswood Nursery, USA
Stonecrop Gardens, USA

CROCOSMIAS (pages 114–121)

SUPPLIERS
Avon Bulbs, England
Blooms of Bressingham, England
The Beth Chatto Gardens, England
Cotswold Garden Flowers, England
Digging Dog Nursery, USA
Forde Abbey Plant Centre, England
Heronswood Nursery, USA
Joy Creek Nursery, USA
R V Roger Ltd, England

COLLECTIONS AND SOCIETIES
Ballyrogan Nursery, Ireland
D&C Fenwick, England
N R Teagle, England

CYCLAMEN (pages 148–155)

SUPPLIERS
Ashwood Nurseries, England
P R Cornish, England
Dicksonia Rare Plants, Australia
Fraser's Thimble Farms, Canada
Russell Graham Purveyor of Plants, USA
Hansen Nursery, USA
Hill View Rare Plants, Australia
Jill White, England
Merry Garth, Australia
Seneca Hill Perennials, USA
Tile Barn Nursery, England

COLLECTIONS AND SOCIETIES
The Cyclamen Society, England
Missouri Botanical Garden, USA
Stonecrop Gardens, USA
Wave Hill, USA

DAPHNES (pages 180–187)

SUPPLIERS
Arrowhead Alpines, USA
Blackthorn Nursery, England
Gossler Farms Nursery, USA
PMA Plant Specialities, England
Quindalup Specialist Nursery, Australia
Siskiyou Rare Plant Nursery, USA
Yamina Rare Plants, Australia

COLLECTIONS AND SOCIETIES
Michael Baron, England
Mrs D Field, England
Gossler Farms Nursery, USA

EREMURUS (pages 80–87)

SUPPLIERS
Jacques Amand Ltd, England
Dicksonia Rare Plants, Australia
Russell Graham Purveyor of Plants, USA
McClure & Zimmerman, USA
RV Roger Ltd, England
John Scheepers Inc, USA
Van Diemen Quality Bulbs, Australia
Van Tubergen UK Ltd, England

COLLECTIONS AND SOCIETIES
Chicago Botanic Garden, USA
Missouri Botanical Garden, USA

EUCOMIS (pages 72–79)

SUPPLIERS
Avon Bulbs, England
Botanicus, England
Brent and Becky's Bulbs, USA
Broersen Bulbs Pty. Ltd, Australia
Cotswold Garden Flowers, England
Crûg Farm Plants, Wales
Plant Delights Nursery, USA
Gary and Sue Reid, Australia
Seneca Hill Perennials, USA

FRITILLARIES (pages 14–21)

SUPPLIERS
Jacques Amand Ltd, England
Avon Bulbs, England
Brent and Becky's Bulbs, USA
Broadleigh Gardens, England
The Beth Chatto Gardens, England
Paul Christian Rare Plants, Wales
Dicksonia Rare Plants, Australia
Hill View Rare Plants, Australia
McClure & Zimmerman, USA
Merry Garth, Australia
Telos Rare Bulbs, USA

COLLECTIONS AND SOCIETIES
Chicago Botanic Garden, USA
Longwood Gardens, USA
Missouri Botanical Garden, USA

GENTIANS (pages 156–163)

SUPPLIERS
Aberconwy Nursery, Wales
Arrowhead Alpines, USA
Christie's Nursery, Scotland
Dicksonia Rare Plants, Australia
Edrom Nurseries, England
Russell Graham Purveyor of Plants, USA
Hartside Nursery, England
Mt. Tahoma Nursery, USA
Plant Hunters Nursery, Australia

COLLECTIONS AND SOCIETIES
The Alpine Garden Society, England
Christie's Nursery, Scotland
Mrs J Ritchie, England
Scottish Rock Garden Club, England
Stonecrop Gardens, USA

GERANIUMS (pages 106–113)

SUPPLIERS
Cally Gardens, Scotland
Cranesbill Nursery, England
Croftway Nursery, England
Crûg Farm Plants, Wales
Fraser's Thimble Farms, Canada
Geraniaceae, USA
Hazlewood Gardens, Australia
Heronswood Nursery, USA
Lambley Nursery, Australia
Rushfields of Ledbury, England
Woodbridge Nursery, Australia

COLLECTIONS AND SOCIETIES
Cambridge University Botanic Garden, England
Catforth Gardens, England
Cherry Hinton Hall Park, England
Chicago Botanic Garden, USA
Coombland Gardens, England
East Lambrook Manor, England
Joy Creek Nursery, USA
Longwood Gardens, USA
Missouri Botanical Garden, USA
Stonecrop Gardens, USA
Wave Hill, USA

HYDRANGEAS (pages 164–171)

SUPPLIERS
Burncoose Nurseries, England
Fillan's Plants, England
Forestfarm, USA
Halecat Garden Nursery, England
Hazlewood Gardens, Australia
Heronswood Nursery, USA
Hydrangeas Plus, USA
Nutlin Nursery, England
Perryhill Nurseries, England
Starborough Nurseries, England
Tesselaar Bulbs & Flowers, Australia
Yamina Rare Plants, Australia

COLLECTIONS AND SOCIETIES
Le Bois des Moutiers, France
Gossler Farms Nursery, USA
Holehird, England
Longwood Gardens, USA
Missouri Botanical Garden, USA
The RHS Garden, Wisley, England
Wave Hill, USA

KNIPHOFIAS (pages 122–129)

SUPPLIERS
Ballyrogan Nurseries, Ireland
Beeches Nursery, England
Canyon Creek Nursery, USA
The Beth Chatto Gardens, England
Cotswold Garden Flowers, England
Digging Dog Nursery, USA
Lambley Nursery, Australia
Seneca Hill Perennials, USA

COLLECTIONS AND SOCIETIES
Joy Creek Nursery, USA
Missouri Botanical Garden, USA
Mount Stewart, Northern Ireland

LAVENDER (pages 64–71)

SUPPLIERS
Arne Herbs, England
Digging Dog Nursery, USA
Goodwin Creek Gardens, USA
Hollington Nurseries, England
Jersey Lavender Ltd, Jersey
Norfolk Lavender, England
Sandy Mush Herb Nursery, USA

COLLECTIONS AND SOCIETIES
Joy Creek Nursery, USA
Matanzas Creek Winery, USA
Yuulong Lavender Estate, Australia

LILIES (pages 48–55)

SUPPLIERS

Jacques Amand Ltd, England
Avon Bulbs, England
B & D Lilies, USA
Broadleigh Gardens, England
Golden Ray Gardens, Australia
The Lily Nook, Canada
Long Acre Plants, England
John Scheepers Inc, USA
Vogelvry Bulbs and Flowers, Australia

COLLECTIONS AND SOCIETIES

Chicago Botanic Garden, USA
Longwood Gardens, USA
Missouri Botanical Garden, USA
North American Lily Society, USA
Quarryhill Botanical Garden, USA

MONARDAS (pages 130–137)

SUPPLIERS

Busse Gardens, USA
Cally Gardens, Scotland
Carroll Gardens, USA
Digger's Club, Australia
Forestfarm, USA
Four Seasons Nursery, England
Honeysuckle Cottage, Australia
Monksilver Nursery, England
Kwekerij Oudolf, The Netherlands

COLLECTIONS AND SOCIETIES

André Viette Farm & Nursery, USA
Chicago Botanic Garden, USA
Missouri Botanical Garden, USA
The RHS Garden, Wisley, England

ORIENTAL POPPIES (pages 98–105)

SUPPLIERS

André Viette Farm & Nursery, USA
Blue Dandenongs Bulb Farm, Australia
Bourdillon Nursery, France

Busse Gardens, USA
The Beth Chatto Gardens, England
Cotswold Garden Flowers, England
Digger's Club, Australia
Earthly Pursuits, USA
Elizabeth Town Nursery, Australia
Four Seasons, England
Pioneer Nursery, England

COLLECTIONS AND SOCIETIES

The Scottish Agricultural College, Scotland
Water Meadow Nursery, England

PASSION FLOWERS (pages 206–213)

SUPPLIERS

Burncoose Nurseries, England
Butterfly World at Tradewinds Park, USA
Glasshouse Works, USA
Kartuz Greenhouses, USA
Logee's Greenhouses, USA
Priorswood Clematis, England
Roseland House Nursery, England
Sherston Parva Nursery, England

COLLECTIONS AND SOCIETIES

Greenholm Nurseries, England
Missouri Botanical Garden, USA
Passiflora Society International, USA

PHORMIUMS (pages 56–63)

SUPPLIERS

Ballyrogon Nursery, Ireland
Burncoose Nurseries, England
Forestfarm, USA
Greer Gardens, USA
Heronswood Nursery, USA
Lambley Nursery, Australia
Plaxtol Nurseries, England
San Marcos Growers, USA

COLLECTIONS AND SOCIETIES

Charney Well, England
Mount Stewart, Northern Ireland

PRIMULAS (pages 30–37)

SUPPLIERS

Ardfearn Nursery, Scotland
Arrowhead Alpines, USA
Blue Dandenongs Bulb Farm, Australia
Botanic Nursery, England
Edrom Nurseries, Scotland
Heronswood Nursery, USA
Honeysuckle Cottage, Australia
Jack Drake, Scotland
Misty Downs, Australia
Mt Tahoma Nursery, USA
Woodbridge Nursery, Australia

COLLECTIONS AND SOCIETIES

Chicago Botanic Garden, USA
Mr D Lochhead, England
Missouri Botanical Garden, USA
National Auricula and Primula Society,
England
Stonecrop Gardens, USA

PROTEAS (pages 198–205)

SUPPLIERS

The Banana Tree, USA
Baxter's Protea Nursery, Australia
Facey's Nursery Pty Ltd, Australia
The Fijnbosch Farme Trust, South Africa
Protea World, Australia
Silverhill Seeds, South Africa
Trevena Cross Nursery, England

COLLECTIONS AND SOCIETIES

Kirstenbosch Botanic Garden, South Africa
Tresco Abbey Gardens, England
University of California, Santa Cruz
(Arboretum), USA

PULMONARIAS (pages 22–29)

SUPPLIERS

All Rare Herbs, Australia
Avondale Nursery, England
Bregover Plants, England
Busse Gardens, USA
Carroll Gardens, USA
The Beth Chatto Gardens, England
Four Seasons Nursery, England
Hazelwood Gardens, Australia
Heronswood Nursery, USA
Lambley Nursery, Australia
Monksilver Nursery, England
Plant Hunters Nursery, Australia
Stillingfleet Lodge Nurseries, England
Wychwood Plants, Australia

COLLECTIONS AND SOCIETIES

Chicago Botanic Garden, USA
Joy Creek Nursery, USA
Longwood Gardens, USA
Missouri Botanical Garden, USA
Stillingfleet Lodge Nurseries, England

SARRACENIAS (pages 190–197)

SUPPLIERS

John Ainsworth, England
Carnivorous and Unusual Seeds, Australia
Dragonfly Aquatics, Australia
Fairweather Gardens, USA
Hampshire Carnivorous Plants, England
Hyde's Stove-House, USA
M King, England
Plant Delights Nursery, USA
South West Carnivorous Plants, England

COLLECTIONS AND SOCIETIES

John Ainsworth, England
Longwood Gardens, USA
Missouri Botanical Garden, USA

SEDUMS (pages 88–95)

SUPPLIERS

Al-Ru Farm Nursery, Australia
Busse Gardens, USA
Cally Gardens, Scotland
Carroll Gardens, USA
The Beth Chatto Gardens, England
Heronswood Nursery, USA
Lambley Nursery, Australia
Monksilver Nursery, England
Potterton & Martin, England
Stillingfleet Lodge Nurseries, England

COLLECTIONS AND SOCIETIES

André Viette Farm & Nursery, USA
Chicago Botanic Garden, USA
Joy Creek Nursery, USA
Longwood Gardens, USA
Missouri Botanical Garden, USA
R Stephenson, England

SIBERIAN IRISES (pages 140–147)

SUPPLIERS

David Austin Roses, England
Draycott Gardens, USA
Eartheart Gardens, USA
Four Seasons Nursery, England
Impressive Irises, Australia
Joe Pye Weed's Garden, USA
Lingen Nursery, England
Mountain View Gardens, USA
Nicholls Gardens, USA
Rainbow Ridge, Australia
Tempo Two, Australia
Tranquil Lake Nursery, USA

COLLECTIONS AND SOCIETIES

American Iris Society, USA
British Iris Society, England
Chicago Botanic Garden, USA
Kim Davis, England
Longwood Gardens, USA

Missouri Botanical Garden, USA
The RHS Garden, Wisley, England
The Royal Botanic Garden, Edinburgh,
Scotland;
Wakehurst Place, England

SNOWDROPS (pages 172–179)

SUPPLIERS

Jacques Amand, England
Avon Bulbs, England
Brent and Becky's Bulbs, USA
Broadleigh Gardens, England
Bulbes d'Opale, France
Dicksonia Rare Plants, Australia
Foxgrove Plants, England
Gardenscape, England
McClure & Zimmerman, USA
North Green Snowdrops, England
Potterton & Martin, England
Raveningham Gardens, England
The Temple Nursery, USA

COLLECTIONS AND SOCIETIES

Anglesey Abbey, England
Michael Baron, England
Benington Lordship, England
La Berquerie, France
David Bromley, England
Chicago Botanic Garden, USA
Heronswood Nursery, USA
Hodsock Priory, England
Longwood Gardens, USA
Missouri Botanical Garden, USA
Painswick Rococo Gardens, England
The RHS Garden, Wisley, England
Stonecrop Gardens, USA
Walsingham Abbey, England

If you are planning to visit a supplier, collection or society, please telephone before you go.

Aberconwy Nursery
Graig, Glan Conwy, Colwyn Bay,
Conwy LL28 5TL, Wales
Tel: + 44 (0)1492 580875
No mail order

John Ainsworth
Bank Farm, Bank Head Lane,
Bamber Bridge, Preston,
Lancs PR5 6YR, England
Tel: +44 (0)1772 321557
Mail order available

All Rare Herbs
Box 91, Mapleton,
Queensland 4560, Australia
Tel: +61 (0)7 5446 9243
E-mail: mcplant@hotmail.com
No mail order

The Alpine Garden Society
Avon Bank, Pershore,
Worcester WR10 3JP, England
Tel: +44 (0)1386 554790
www.alpinegardensociety.org
Mail order available

Al-Ru Farm Nursery
PO Box 270, One Tree Hill,
South Australia 5114
Tel: +61 (0)8 8280 7353
E-mail: ruthirving@hotmail.com
Mail order available; Australia only

Jacques Amand Ltd
The Nurseries, 145 Clamp Hill,
Stanmore, Middx HA7 3JS, England
Tel: +44 (0)20 8954 8138
E-mail: bulbs@jacquesamand.co.uk
Mail order available

American Iris Society
Marilyn Harlow, Dept. E,
PO Box 55, Freedom,
CA 95019, USA
www.irises.org
Mail order available

Anglesey Abbey
Lode, Cambridgeshire CB5 9EJ,
England
Tel:+44 (0)1223 811200
www.nationaltrust.org/angleseyabbey
No mail order

Ardfearn Nursery
Bunchrew, Inverness IV3 8RH,
Scotland
Tel: +44 (0)1463 243250
E-mail: ardfearn@tinyworld.com
Mail order available

Arne Herbs
Limeburn Nurseries, Limeburn Hill,
Chew Magna, Avon BS40 8QW,
England
Tel: +44 (0)1275 333399
www.arneherbs.co.uk
Mail order available

Arrowhead Alpines
PO Box 857, Fowlerville
MI 48836, USA
Tel: +1 517 223 3581
www.arrowheadalpines.com
Mail order available; US only

Ashwood Nurseries
Ashwood Lower Lane,
Ashwood, Kingswinford,
W Midlands DY6 OAE, England
Tel: +44 (0)1384 401996
www.ashwood-nurseries.co.uk
No mail order

David Austin Roses
Bowling Green Lane, Albrighton,
Wolverhampton WV7 3HB,
England
Tel: +44 (0)1902 376300
www.davidaustinroses.com
Mail order available

Avon Bulbs
Burnt House Farm,
Mid Lambrook, South Petherton,
Somerset TA13 5HE, England
Tel: +44 (0)1460 242177
www.avonbulbs.com
Mail order available; Europe only

Avondale Nursery
3 Avondale Road, Earlsden,
Coventry CV5 6DZ, England
Tel: +44 (0)2476 673662
www.avondalenursery.co.uk
Mail order available

B&D Lilies
PO Box 2007, Port Townsend
WA 98368, USA
Tel: +1 360 765 4341
www.bdlilies.com
Mail order available; US only

Ballyrogan Nurseries
The Grange, 35 Ballyrogan Park,
Newtonards, Co Down BT23 4SD,
Ireland
Tel: +44 (0)2891 810451
Mail order available

The Banana Tree
717 Northampton Street, Easton
PA 18042, USA
Tel: +1 610 253 9589
www.banana-tree.com
Mail order available

Michael Baron
Brandy Mount House, Alresford,
Hants SO24 9EG, England
Tel: +44 (0)1962 732189
www.brandymount.co.uk
No mail order

Baxter's Protea Nursery
14 Merryn Court, Narangba,
Queensland 4504, Australia
Tel: +61 (0)7 3888 2909

Beeches Nursery
Village Centre, Ashdon, Saffron
Walden, Essex CB10 2HB, England
Tel: +44 (0)1799 584362
www.beechesnursery.co.uk
Mail order available; UK only

Benington Lordship
Benington, near Stevenage,
Hertfordshire SG2 7BS, England
Tel: +44 (0)1438 869668
www.beningtonlordship.co.uk
No mail order

La Berquerie
Route du Manoir d'Ango, 76119
Varengeville-sur-Mer, France
Tel: +33 2 35 85 13 10

Blackthorn Nursery
Kilmeston, Alresford,
Hants SO24 0NL, England
Tel: +44 (0)1692 771796
No mail order

Blooms of Bressingham
Bressingham, Diss,
Norfolk IP22 2AB, England
Tel: +44 (0)1379 688585
Mail order available; UK only

Blue Dandenongs Bulb Farm
Old Emerald Road, Monbulk,
Victoria 3793, Australia
Tel: +61 (0)3 9756 6766
www.blued.com.au
Mail order; Australia only

Le Bois des Moutiers
Rue de l'Eglise, Varengeville-sur-
Mer, Seine Maritime, France
Tel: +33 2 35 85 10 02

The Botanic Garden
41319 Gothenburg, Sweden
Tel: +46 31 41 81 12

The Botanic Nursery
Cottles Lane, Atworth,
Wilts SN12 8NU, England
www.thebotanicnursery.com
Mail order available; Europe only

Botanicus
The Nurseries, Ringland Lane,
Old Costessey, Norwich,
Norfolk NR8 5BG, England
Tel: +44 (0)1603 742063
E-mail: doffo@tiscali.co.uk
Mail order available; Europe only

Bourdillon Nursery
BP2 41230, Soings en Sologne,
France
Tel: + 33 2 54 98 71 06
www.bourdillon.com
Mail order available

Bregover Plants
Hillbrooke, Middlewood, North Hill,
Cornwall PL15 7NN, England
Tel: +44 (0)1566 782661
Mail order available; UK only

Brent and Becky's Bulbs
7463 Heath Trail, Gloucester
VA 23061, USA
Tel: +1 804 693 3966
E-mail:
info@brentandbeckysbulbs.com
Mail order available; US only

British Iris Society
Mr E H Furnival,
15 Parkwood Drive, Rawtenstall,
Lancashire BB4 6RP, England

Broadleigh Gardens
Bishops Hull, Taunton,
Somerset TA4 1AE, England
Tel: +44 (0)1823 286231
www.broadleighbulbs.co.uk
Mail order available; Europe only

Broersen Bulbs Pty Ltd
365–367 Monbulk Road, Silvan,
Victoria 3795, Australia
Tel: +61 (0)3 9737 9202
E-mail: sales@broersen.com.au
Mail order available; Australia only

David Bromley
Moortown, nr Wellington,
Shrops TF6 6JE, England
No mail order

Bulbes d'Opale
384 Boerenweg Ouest, 59285
Buysscheure Nord, France
Tel: +33 3 28 43 04 67
Mail order available

Burncoose Nurseries
Gwennap, Redruth,
Cornwall TR16 6BJ, England
Tel: +44 (0)1209 861112
www.burncoose.co.uk
Mail order available

Busse Gardens
17160 245th Avenue,
Big Lake MN 55309, USA
Tel: +1 800 544 3192
www.bussegardens.com
Mail order available; US only

**Butterfly World at
Tradewinds Park**
3600 West Sample Road, Coconut
Creek, Florida FL 33073, USA
Tel: +1 954 977 4400
www.butterflyworld.com
No mail order

Cally Gardens
Gatehouse of Fleet, Castle Douglas
DG7 2DJ, Scotland
Tel: +44 (0)1557 815029
www.fsperennials.co.uk
Mail order available

**Cambridge University
Botanic Garden**
Cory Lodge, Bateman Street,
Cambridge CB2 1JF, England
Tel: +44 (0)1223 336265
www.botanic.cam.ac.uk
No mail order

Canyon Creek Nursery
3527 Dry Creek Road, Oroville
CA 95965, USA
Tel: +1 530 533 2166
www.canyoncreeknursery.com
Mail order available; US only

Carnivorous and Unusual Seeds
3 Normanby Avenue, Para Hills,
South Australia 5096
Tel: +61 (0)8 8264 2825
Mail order available; Australia only

Carroll Gardens
444 East Main Street,
Westminster MD 21157, USA
Tel: +1 800 638 6334
www.carrollgardens.com
Mail order available; US only

Catforth Gardens
Roots Lane, Catforth, Preston,
Lancs PR4 0JB, England
Tel: +44 (0)1772 690561
No mail order

Charney Well
Hampsfell Road, Grange-over-
Sands, Cumbria LA11 6BE, England
Tel: +44 (0)15395 34526

The Beth Chatto Gardens
Elmstead Market, Colchester,
Essex CO7 7DB, England
Tel: +44 (0)1206 822007
www.bethchatto.co.uk
Mail order available; Europe only

Cherry Hinton Hall Park
Cherry Hinton Hall Road,
Cambridge CB1 4DW, England
Tel: +44 (0)1223 411506
No mail order

Chicago Botanic Garden
1000 Lake Cook Road,
Glencoe IL 60022, USA
Tel: +1 847 835 5440
www.chicago-botanic.org

Paul Christian Rare Plants
PO Box 468, Wrexham, Clwyd
LL13 9XR, Wales
Tel: +44 (0)1978 366399
www.rareplants.co.uk
Mail order available

Christie's Nursery
Downfield, Main Road, Westmuir,
Kirriemuir, Angus DD8 5LP,
Scotland
Tel: +44 (0)1575 572977
www.christiealpines.co.uk
Mail order available

Coombland Gardens
Coneyhurst, Billingshurst, W Sussex
RH14 9DG, England
Tel: +44 (0)1403 741727
www.coombland.co.uk
Mail order available

P R Cornish
116 Oxtalls Lane, Longlevens,
Gloucs GL2 9HY, England
Tel: +44 (0)1452 520004
Mail order available; UK only

Cotswold Garden Flowers
Sands Lane, Badsey, Evesham,
Worcs WR11 5EZ, England
Tel: +44 (0)1386 422829
www.cgf.net
Mail order available

Cranesbill Nursery
White Cottage, Stock Green,
nr Redditch, Worcs B96 6SZ
England
Tel: +44 (0)1386 792414
E-mail: fmandjbates@aol.com
Mail order available; Europe only

Croftway Nursery
Yapton Road, Barnham, Bognor
Regis, W Sussex PO22 0BQ,
England
Tel: +44 (0)1243 552121
www.croftway.co.uk
Mail order available

Crûg Farm Plants
Griffith's Crossing, nr Caernarfon,
Gwynedd LL55 1TU, Wales
Tel: +44 (0)1248 670232
www.crug-farm.co.uk
No mail order

The Cyclamen Society
Secretary PJM Moore, Tile Barn
House, Standen Street, Iden Green,
Benenden, Kent TN17 4LB,
England
www.cyclamen.org

Dicksonia Rare Plants
684 Mount Macedon Road, Mount
Macedon, Victoria 3441, Australia
Tel: +61 (0)3 5426 3075
No mail order

Digger's Club
105 Latrobe Parade, Dromana,
Victoria 3936, Australia
Tel: +61 (0)3 5987 1877
www.diggers.com.au
Mail order available; Australia only

Digging Dog Nursery
PO Box 471, Albion CA 95410,
USA
Tel: +1 707 937 1130
www.diggingdog.com
Mail order available; US only

Dragonfly Aquatics
RMB Apollo Bay 366, via Colac,
Victoria 3249, Australia
Tel: +61 (0)3 5236 6320
Mail order available; Australia only

Jack Drake
Inshriach Alpine Nursery, Aviemore,
Invernesshire PH22 1QS, Scotland
Tel: +44 (0)1540 651287
www.drakesalpines.com
No mail order

Draycott Gardens
16815 Falls Road, Upperco
MD 21155, USA
Tel: +1 410 374 4788
www.gardeneureka.com/drayc/

Eartheart Gardens
RR 1, Box 847, South Harpswell
ME 044079, USA
Tel: +1 207 833 6327

Earthly Pursuits
2901 Kuntz Road, Windsor Mill
MD 21244, USA
Tel: +1 410 496 2523
www.earthlypursuits.net
Mail order available; US only

East Lambrook Manor
South Petherton,
Somerset TA13 5HL, England
Tel: +44 (0)1460 240328
www.eastlambrook.com
Mail order available

Edrom Nurseries
Coldingham, Eyemouth,
Berwickshire TD14 5TZ, Scotland
Tel: +44 (0)1890 771386
www.edromnurseries.co.uk
Mail order available

Elizabeth Town Nursery
5988 Bass Highway, Deloraine,
Tasmania 7304, Australia
Tel: +61 (0)3 6368 1192
Email: hortus@microtech.com.au
No mail order

Facey's Nursery Pty Ltd
1870 South Gippsland Highway,
Cranbourne, Victoria 3977,
Australia
Tel: +61 (0)3 5996 1466
No mail order

Fairweather Gardens
PO Box 330, Greenwich NJ 08323,
USA
Tel: +1 956 451 6261
www.fairweathergardens.com
Mail order available; US only

D&C Fenwick
The African Garden, 96 Wasdale
Gardens, Estover, Plymouth,
Devon PL6 8TW, England
Tel: +44 (0)1752 301402
www.theafricangarden.com
No mail order

Mrs D Field
42 Park Lane, Hartford, Northwich,
Cheshire CW8 1PZ, England
Tel: +44 (0)1606 75642
E-mail: pauldenise@talk21.com
No mail order

The Fijnbosch Farme Trust
PO Box 26445, 7872 Hout Bay,
South Africa
Tel: +27 21 701 8231
www.finebushpeople.co.za
Mail order available

Fillan's Plants
Tucker Marsh Gardens, Tamar Lane,
Bere Alston, Devon PL20 7HN,
England
Tel: +44 (0)1822 840721
E-mail: fillansplants@yahoo.co.uk
Mail order available; UK only

Forde Abbey Plant Centre
Forde Abbey, Chard, Somerset
TA20 4LU, England
Tel: +44 (0)1460 220088
www.fordeabbey.co.uk
No mail order

Forestfarm
990 Tetherow Road, Williams
OR 97544, USA
Tel: +1 541 846 7269
www.forestfarm.com
Mail order available; US only

Four Seasons Nursery
Forncett St Mary, Norwich,
Norfolk NR16 1JT, England
Tel: +44 (0)1508 488344
www.fsperennials.co.uk
Mail order available: Europe only

Foxgrove Plants
Enborne, nr Newbury,
Berks RG14 6RE, England
Tel: +44 (0)1635 40554
Mail order available; UK only

Fraser's Thimble Farms
175 Arbutus Road, Salt Spring Island
BC V8K 1A3, Canada
Tel: +1 250 537 5788
www.thimblefarms.com
Mail order available

Gardenscape
Fairview, Smelthouses,
Summerbridge, Harrogate,
N Yorks HG3 4DH, England
Tel: +44 (0)1423 780291
www.gardenscape.co.uk
Mail order available; Europe only

Geraniaceae
122 Hillcrest Avenue,
Kentfield CA 94904, USA
Tel: +1 415 461 4168
www.geraniaceae.com
Mail order available; US only

Glasshouse Works
PO Box 97, Stewart OH 45778,
USA
Tel: +1 740 662 2142
www.glasshouseworks.com
Mail order available; US only

Golden Ray Gardens
1 Monash Avenue, Olinda,
Victoria 3788, Australia
Tel: +61 (0)3 9751 1395
E-mail: sales@goldenray.com.au
Mail order available; Australia only

Goodwin Creek Gardens
PO Box 83, Williams
OR 97544, USA
Tel: +1 800 846 7359
www.goodwincreekgardens.com
Mail order available; US only

Gossler Farms Nursery
1200 Weaver Road, Springfield
OR 97478, USA
Tel: +1 541 746 3922
Mail order available

Russell Graham Purveyor of Plants
4030 Eagle Crest Road NW,
Salem OR 97304, USA
Tel: +1 503 362 1135
Email: grahams@open.org
Mail order available; US only

Greenholm Nurseries
Lampley Road, Kingston Seymour,
Clevedon, BS21 6XS, England
Tel: +44 (0)1934 833350
www.passiflora-uk.co.uk
Mail order available

Greer Gardens
1280 Goodpasture Island Road,
Eugene OR 97401, USA
Tel: +1 541 686 8266
www.greergardens.com
Mail order available

Halecat Garden Nursery
The Yard, 1 Halecat Cottages,
Witherslack, Cumbria LA11 6RT,
England
Tel: +44 (0)1539 552536
www.halecat.co.uk
Mail order available; Europe only

Hampshire Carnivorous Plants
Ya-mayla, Allington Lane, West End,
Southampton SO30 3HQ, England
Tel: +44 (0)2380 473314
www.hampshire-carnivorous.co.uk
Mail order available; Europe only

Hansen Nursery
PO Box 1228, North Bend,
Oregon OR 97459, USA
Tel: +1 541 756 1156
E-mail: hansen.nursery@verizon.net

Hartside Nursery Garden
nr Alston, Cumbria CA9 3BL,
England
Tel: +44 (0)1434 381372
E-mail: hartside@mac.unlimited.net
Mail order available; Europe only

Hazelwood Gardens
Ferguson Crescent, Mittagong,
NSW 2575, Australia
Tel +61 (0)2 4872 2458
Mail order available; Australia only

Heronswood Nursery
7530 NE 288th Street, Kingston
WA 98346, USA
Tel: +1 360 297 4172
www.heronswood.com
Mail order available

Hill View Rare Plants
400 Huon Road, South Hobart,
Tasmania 7004, Australia
Tel: +61 (0)3 6224 0770
Mail order available; Australia only

Hodsock Priory
Blyth, near Worksop,
Nottinghamshire S81 0TY, England
Tel: +44 (0)1909 591204
www.snowdrops.co.uk
No mail order

Holehird
Patterdale Road, Windermere,
Cumbria LA23 1NP, England
Tel: +44 (0)15394 46008
www.cragview.demon.co.uk
No mail order

Hollington Nurseries
Woolton Hill, Newbury,
Berks RG15 9XT, England
Tel: +44 (0)1635 253908
Mail order available

Honeysuckle Cottage
Lot 35, Bowen Mountain Road,
Bowen Mountain, NSW 2753,
Australia
Tel: +61 (0)2 4572 1345
No mail order

Hyde's Stove-House
844 37th Avenue S,
St. Petersburg FL 33705, USA
www.stovehouseplants.com
Mail order available; US only

Hydrangeas Plus
PO Box 389, Aurora
OR 97002, USA
Tel: +1 866 433 7896
www.hydrangeasplus.com
Mail order available; US only

Hythe Alpines
Methwold Hythe, Thetford,
Norfolk IP26 4QH, England
Tel: +44 (0)1366 728543
E-mail: mike.hythealpines@
tinyworld.co.uk
Mail order available; Europe only

Impressive Irises
PO Box 169, Charleston,
South Australia 5244, Australia
Tel +61 (0)8 8389 4439
E-mail: irises@senet.com.au
Mail order available; Australia only

Jersey Lavender Ltd
Rue du Pont Marquet,
St Brelade JE3 8DS, Jersey
Tel: +44 (0)1534 742933
www.jerseylavender.co.uk
Mail order available

Joy Creek Nursery
20300 NW Watson Road,
Scappoose OR 97056, USA
Tel: +1 503 543 7474
www.joycreek.com
Mail order available

Kartuz Greenhouses
PO Box 790, Vista CA 92085, USA
Tel: +1 760 941 3613
www.kartuz.com
Mail order available; US only

M King
5 Field Close, Malinslee, Telford,
Shrops TF4 2EH, England
Tel: +44 (0)1952 501598

Kirstenbosch Botanic Garden
Rhodes Drive, Private Bag X7,
Claremont, South Africa
Tel: +27 21 799 8899
www.nbi.ac.za
No mail order

Lambley Nursery
Burnside, Lesters Road, Ascot,
Victoria 3364, Australia
Tel: +61 (0)3 5343 4303
www.lambley.com.au
Mail order available; Australia only

The Lily Nook
Box 846, Neepawa,
MB R0J 1H0, Canada
Tel: +1 204 476 3225
www.lilynook.mb.ca
Mail order available

Lingen Nursery
Lingen, Bucknell, Shrops SY7 0DY,
England
Tel: +44 (0)1544 267720
www.lingennursery.co.uk
Mail order available; UK only

Mr D Lochhead
Field House Alpines, Leake Road,
Gotham, Notts NG11 0JN, England
Tel: +44 (0)1159 830278
Mail order available

Long Acre Plants
Charlton Musgrove, nr Wincanton,
Somerset BA9 8EX, England
Tel: +44 (0)1963 32802
www.longacreplants.co.uk

Longwood Gardens
PO Box 501, Kennett Square
PA 19348, USA
Tel: +1 610 388 1000
www.longwoodgardens.com

Matanzas Creek Winery
6097 Bennett Valley Road,
Santa Rosa CA 95404, USA
Tel: +1 800 590 6464
www.matanzascreek.com

McClure & Zimmerman
PO Box 368, 108 W Winnebago,
Freisland WI 53935, USA
Tel: +1 800 883 6998
www.mzbulb.com
Mail order available; US only

Merry Garth
Davies Lane, Mount Wilson,
NSW 2786, Australia
Tel: +61 (0)2 4756 2121
No mail order

Missouri Botanical Garden
PO Box 299, St. Louis
MO 63166, USA
Tel: +1 800 642 8842
www.mobot.org

Misty Downs
515 Daylesford-Clunes Road,
Kingston, Victoria 3364, Australia
Tel: +61 (0)3 5345 6575
Mail order available; Australia only

Monksilver Nursery
Oakington Road, Cottenham,
Cambridge, Cambs CB4 8TW,
England
Tel: +44 (0)1954 251555
www.monksilver.com
Mail order available

Mount Stewart
Greyabbey, Newtonards BT22 2AD,
Northern Ireland
Tel: +44 (0)28 4278 8387
No mail order

Mountain View Gardens
2435 Middle Road, Columbia Falls
MT 59912, USA
Tel: +1 406 892 5020
www.mountainviewgardens.com/

Mt Tahoma Nursery
28111 112th Avenue E,
Graham WA 98338, USA
Tel: +1 253 847 9827
www.backyardgardener.com/
mttahoma/
Mail order available; US only

**National Auricula and
Primula Society**
67 Warnham Court Road,
Carshalton Beeches,
Surrey SM15 3ND, England
www.auriculaandprimula.org.uk

Nicholls Gardens
4724 Angus Drive, Gainesville
VA 20155, USA
Tel: +1 703 754 9623

Norfolk Lavender
Caley Hill, Heacham, King's Lynn,
Norfolk PE31 7JE, England
Tel: +44 (0)1485 70384
www.norfolk-lavender.co.uk
Mail order available

North American Lily Society
PO Box 272, Owatonna,
Minnesota MN 55060, USA
Tel: +1 507 451 2170
www.lilies.org

North Green Snowdrops
North Green Only, Stoven, Beccles,
Suffolk NR34 8DG, England
Mail order available

Nutlin Nursery
Crowborough Road, Nutley,
Uckfield, E Sussex TN22 3HH,
England
Tel: +44 (0)1825 712670
No mail order

Kwekerij Oudolf
Broekstraat 17, 6999
DE Hummerlo, The Netherlands
Tel: +31 8348 1120

Painswick Rococo Gardens
Painswick, near Stroud,
Gloucestershire GL6 6TH, England
Tel: +44 (0)1452 813204
www.rococogarden.co.uk
No mail order

Paradise Centre
Twinstead Road, Lamarsh, Bures,
Suffolk CO8 5EX, England
Tel: +44 (0)1787 269449
www.paradisecentre.com
Mail order available; Europe only

Passiflora Society International
c/o Butterfly World, 3600 Sample
Road, Coconut Creek FL 33073,
USA
Email: azinno@aol.com

Perryhill Nurseries Ltd
Edenbridge Road, Hartfield,
E Sussex TN7 4JP, England
Tel: +44 (0)1892 770377
www.perryhillnurseries.co.uk
Mail order available; UK only

Pioneer Nursery
Baldock Lane, Willian, Letchworth,
Herts SG6 2AE, England
Tel: +44 (0)1462 675858
www.pioneerplants.com
Mail order available

Plant Delights Nursery
9241 Sauls Road, Raleigh
NC 27603, USA
Tel: +1 919 772 4794
www.plantdelights.com
Mail order available

Plant Hunters Nursery
1115 Huon Road, Neika,
Tasmania 7054, Australia
Tel: +61 (0)3 6239 1401
Mail order available; Australia only

Plaxtol Nurseries
Plaxtol, Sevenoaks,
Kent TN15 0QR, England
Tel: +44 (0)1732 810550
www.plaxtol-nurseries.co.uk
Mail order available; UK only

PMA Plant Specialities
Junker's Nursery Ltd, Lower Mead,
West Hatch, Taunton,
Somerset TA3 5RN, England
Tel: +44 (0)1823 480774
www.junker.net
Mail order available; Europe only

Potterton & Martin
Moortown Road, Nettleton,
Caistor, Lincs LN7 6HX, England
Tel: +44 (0)1472 851714
E-mail: rob@pottertons.co.uk
Mail order available

Priorswood Clematis
Priorswood, Widbury Hill, Ware,
Herts SG12 7QH, England
Tel: +44 (0)1920 461543
Mail order available

Protea World
RSD 1130 Yundi Road, via
Willunga, South Australia 5172
Tel: +61 (0)8 5556 0274
No mail order

Joe Pye Weed's Garden
337 Acton Street,
Carlisle MA 01741, USA
Tel: +1 978 371 0173
www.geocities.com/jpwflowers/
Mail order available; US only

Quarryhill Botanical Garden
PO Box 232, Glen Ellen
CA 95442, USA
Tel: +1 707 996 3802
www.quarryhillbg.org

Quindalup Specialist Nursery
Sproules Lane, Bowral, NSW 2576,
Australia
Tel: +61 (0)2 488 1254
No mail order

Rainbow Ridge
8 Taylors Road, Dural NSW 2158,
Australia
Tel: +61 (0)2 9651 2857
E-mail:
rainbowridge@ozemail.com.au
Mail order available; Australia only

Raveningham Gardens
Norwich, Norfolk NR14 6NS,
England
Tel: +44 (0)1508 548222
www.raveningham.com
Mail order available

Garry & Sue Reid
RMB 6270, via Wodonga,
Victoria 3691, Australia
Tel: +61 (0)2 60 27 1541
Mail order available; Australia only

Red's Rhodies
15920 SW Oberst Lane, Sherwood,
Oregon OR 97140, USA
Tel: +1 503 625 6331

Mrs J Ritchie
Hoo House, Gloucester Road,
Tewkesbury, Glos GL20 7DA,
England
Tel: +44 (0)1684 293389
E-mail: nursery@hoohouse.co.uk
No mail order

Roseland House Nursery
Chacewater, Truro,
Cornwall TR4 8QB, England
Tel: +44 (0)1872 560451
www.roselandhouse.co.uk
Mail order available; UK only

The Royal Botanic Garden
Edinburgh, 20a Inverleith Row,
Edinburgh EH3 5LR, Scotland
Tel: +44 (0)131 552 7171
www.rbge.org.uk
No mail order

**The Royal Horticultural Society
(RHS)**
80 Vincent Square, London
SW1P 2PE, England
Tel: +44 (0)20 7834 4333
www.rhs.org.uk
RHS Plant Finder: The recognised
authority on plant nomenclature.
Listing over 70,000 plants and the
contact details of over 800 nurseries
and suppliers, it is the most
comprehensive directory of the
plants that are available in the UK.
www.rhs.org.uk/rhsplantfinder
AGM: This stands for Award of
Garden Merit, which is given to
outstanding garden plants and is
one of the highest accolades
awarded by the RHS.

**The Royal Horticultural Society
Garden**
Wisley, Surrey GU23 6QB, England
Tel: +44 (0)1483 224234
www.rhs.org.uk
No mail order

Janis Ruksans Bulb Nursery
Rozula, LV-4150 Cesu distr., Latvia
Tel: 011 371 941 8440
Mail order available

Rushfields of Ledbury
Ross Road, Ledbury, Herefordshire
HR8 2LP, England
Tel: +44 (0)1531 632004
www.rushfields.co.uk
No mail order

R V Roger Ltd
The Nurseries, Pickering,
N Yorks YO18 8EA, England
Tel: +44 (0)1751 472226
www.rvroger.co.uk
Mail order available; UK only

San Marcos Growers
125 South San Marcos Road, Santa
Barbara, California CA 93111, USA
Tel: +1 805 683 1561
Email: sales@smgrowers.com

Sandy Mush Herb Nursery
316 Surrett Cove Road,
Leicester NC 2874, USA
Tel: +1 828 683 2014
www.brwm.org/sandymushherbs
Mail order available; US only

John Scheepers Inc
PO Box 638, Bantam,
Connecticut CT 06750, USA
Tel: +1 860 567 0838
www.johnscheepers.com
Mail order available; US only

**The Scottish Agricultural
College**
Auchincruive, Ayr,
Ayrshire KA6 5HW, Scotland
Tel: +44 (0)1292 525393
E-mail: m.hitchon@au.sac.ac.uk
No mail order

Scottish Rock Garden Club
Subscription Secretary, c/o Dickens
Lane, Pynton, Cheshire SK12 1NT,
England
www.srgc.org.uk
No mail order

Seneca Hill Perennials
3712 County Route 57,
Oswego NY 13126, USA
Tel: +1 315 342 5915
www.senecahill.com
Mail order available; US only

Sherston Parva Nursery
Malmesbury Road, Sherston,
Wilts SN16 0NX, England
Tel: +44 (0)1666 841066
www.sherstonparva.com
Mail order available; Europe only

Silverhill Seeds
PO Box 53108, Kenilworth, 7745
Capetown, South Africa
Tel: +27 21 762 4245
www.silverhillseeds.co.za
Mail order available

Siskiyou Rare Plant Nursery
2825 Cummings Road,
Medford OR 97501, USA
Tel: +1 541 772 6846
www.siskiyourareplantnursery.com
Mail order available; US and
Canada only

South West Carnivorous Plants
2 Rose Cottages, Millmoor,
Culmstock, Cullompton,
Devon EX15 3JJ, England
Tel: +44 (0)1884 841549
www.littleshopofhorrors.co.uk
Mail order available; Europe only

Starborough Nurseries
Starborough Road, Marsh Green,
Edenbridge, Kent TN8 5RB,
England
Tel: +44 (0)1732 865614
Mail order available; UK only

R Stephenson
8 Percy Gardens, Choppington,
Northumberland NE62 5YH,
England
Tel: +44 (0) 1670 817901
No mail order

Stillingfleet Lodge Nurseries
Stillingfleet, Yorks YO4 6HW,
England
Tel: +44 (0)1904 728506
www.stillingfleetlodgenurseries.co.uk
Mail order; UK only
(November–March)

Stonecrop Gardens
81 Stonecrop Lane,
Cold Spring NY 10516, USA
Tel: +1 845 265 2000
www.stonecrop.org

N R Teagle
The National Trust,
Lanhydrock Gardens, Bodmin,
Cornwall PL30 5AD, England
Tel: +44 (0)1208 72220
No mail order

Telos Rare Bulbs
PO Box 4978, Arcata CA 95518,
USA
Mail order available

The Temple Nursery
PO Box 591, Trumansburg
NY 14886, USA
Mail order available; US only

Tempo Two
57 East Road, Pearcedale,
Victoria 3912, Australia
Tel: +61 (0)3 5978 6980
Mail order available; Australia only

Tesselaar Bulbs & Flowers
357 Monbulk Road, Silvan,
Victoria 3795, Australia
Tel: +61 (0)3 9737 9811
www.tesselaar.net.au
Mail order available; Australia only

Tile Barn Nursery
Standen Street, Iden Green,
Benenden, Kent TN17 4LB,
England
Tel: +44 (0)1580 240221
www.tilebarn-cyclamen.co.uk
Mail order available

Tranquil Lake Nursery
45 River Street, Rehoboth
MA 02769, USA
Tel: +1 518 252 4002
www.tranquil-lake.com
Mail order available; US only

Tresco Abbey Gardens
Isles of Scilly, Cornwall TR24 0QQ,
England
Tel: +44 (0)1720 424105
www.tresco.co.uk
No mail order

Trevena Cross Nursery
Breage, Helston,
Cornwall TR13 9PS, England
Tel: +44 (0)1736 763880
www.trevenacross.co.uk
Mail order available; UK only

University of California
Santa Cruz (Arboretum),
1156 High Street, Santa Cruz
CA 95064, USA
Tel: +1 831 427 2998
www.ucsc.edu.arboretum/index.html

Van Diemen Quality Bulbs
363 Lighthouse Road, Wynyard,
Tasmania 7325, Australia
Tel: +61 (0)3 6442 2012
Email: vdqbulbs@tassie.net.au
Mail order available; Australia only

Van Tubergen UK Ltd
Bressingham, Diss,
Norfolk IP22 2AG, England
Tel: +44 (0)1379 688282
www.vantubergen.co.uk
Mail order; UK only

André Viette Farm & Nursery
PO Box 1109, Fishersville
VA 22939, USA
Tel: +1 800 575 5538
www.viette.com
Mail order available; US only

Vogelvry Bulbs and Flowers
PO Box 369, New Norfolk,
Tasmania 7140, Australia
Tel: +61 (0)3 6261 3153
www.vogelvry@primus.com.au
Mail order available; Australia only

Wakehurst Place
Ardingly, W Sussex RH17 6TN,
England
Tel: +44 (0)1444 894000
www.kew.org
No mail order

Walsingham Abbey
Walsingham, Norfolk NR22 6BP,
England
Tel: +44 (0)1328 820259
No mail order

Water Meadow Nursery
Cheriton, nr Alresford,
Hants SO24 0QB, England
Tel: +44 (0)1962 771895
www.plantaholic.co.uk
Mail order available

Wave Hill
675 West 252nd Street,
Bronx NY 10471, USA
Tel: +1 718 549 3200
www.wavehill.org

Jill White
6 Edward Avenue, Brightlingsea,
Essex CO7 0LZ, England
Mail order available

Woodbridge Nursery
PO Box 90, Woodbridge,
Tasmania 7162, Australia
Tel: +61 (0)3 6267 4437
Mail order available; Australia only
(March–October)

Wychwood Plants
80 Den Road, Mole Creek,
Tasmania 7304, Australia
Tel: +61 (0)3 6363 1210
Email: cooper-hall@tassie.net.au
Mail order available; Australia only

Yamina Rare Plants
25 Moores Rd, Monbulk, Victoria
3793, Australia
Tel: +61 (0)3 9765 6335
No mail order

Yuulong Lavender Estate
RMB E1215, Ballarat, Victoria
3352, Australia
Tel: +61 (0)3 5368 9453
www.lavender-centre.com
No mail order

JOHN AINSWORTH and his late wife Jean received no formal training in horticulture. While looking for unusual plants to interest children about 30 years ago, they became fascinated by the challenge of growing them. They developed a special interest in insectivorous plants and exhibited at Royal Horticultural Society shows and others, for many years. Their National Collection of *Sarracenia* was awarded scientific status in 1998.

John and Jean were members of many horticultural societies, including the North West Group of the NCCPG and the Royal Horticultural Society. John has also been a member of the NCCPG National Council and the Plant Conservation Committee. Together, John and Jean published a booklet on *Sarracenia* culture, as well as an article in *Curtis's Botanical Magazine*, and gave many lectures on specialist groups of plants and gardening in general.

Today John continues to care for the plant collection and garden with his present wife, Jhansi. Although private, both the garden and the collection are occasionally open to the public.

RUPERT BOWLBY started in the bulb world in the 1960s, as the English Director of Van Tubergen B.V., who have nurseries in Haarlem and Hemstede in Holland, and own a world-famous collection of bulbs, including many from South Africa. During the 15 years he worked there, the firm won 14 Gold Medals at the Chelsea Flower Show, as well as many other accolades.

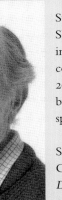

In 1985, Rupert set up his own small bulb nursery in Surrey and exhibited his own plants at the Chelsea Flower Show – and other shows – where he won a Gold Medal in 1993 with a display of over 100 species of *Allium*. After concentrating on his *Allium* collection for many years, in 2002 Rupert turned his nursery over to South African bulbs. His collection now numbers more than 600 different species and varieties and is growing steadily each year.

Rupert has given talks to the Royal Horticultural Society, as well as to the English Gardening School at the Chelsea Physic Garden. He has contributed to *The RHS Dictionary of Gardening* and written articles for the gardening press on a variety of 'bulbous' subjects.

MARK BROWN's earliest memories are of plants in the wild – he began gardening at the age of five and has been passionate about nature since meeting the great amateur naturalist, Susan Cowdy. At the age of 17 he began his botanical travels around the world, including trips to the Soviet Union and central Asia.

In 1999 Mark published his book, *Les Jardins des Champs – Le Souffle de la Nature* and in 1993 he collaborated with D Brunner on the design for the Cabot-Perry Gardens of Giverny. He has also written various articles on meadows and wildflowers.

Mark lives in France, tending the garden at 'La Berquerie', which has wildflower meadows, as well as areas inspired by the architecture and history of the region. He is currently researching the evolution of flowering plants and hopes to create a new garden with primitive plants and reconstitutions of creataceous forests.

Born in 1923, **BETH CHATTO** began her career demonstrating flower arranging. Inspired by her husband, Andrew Chatto (a fruit farmer who studied the natural associations of plants), and her friend, Sir Cedric Morris (the painter and plantsman), she created the celebrated garden at White Barn House in Elmstead. Beth opened her nursery for unusual plants in 1967, which is now one of the most renowned in the world.

A keen advocate of organic gardening, Beth is largely responsible for introducing ecology into modern garden design through her use of plants in natural groupings. Her displays at the Chelsea Flower Show have won her numerous gold medals, including the RHS Lawrence Memorial Medal. In 1998 Beth received a Lifetime Achievement Award from the Garden Writers' Guild and in 2002 she was awarded the OBE for her services to horticulture.

Beth has lectured all over the world and has written numerous articles for international magazines and newspapers. She is also the author of eight books, including *The Dry Garden* (1978), *The Damp Garden* (1982), *Dear Friend and Gardener* (1998) with Christopher Lloyd, *Beth Chatto's Gravel Garden* (2000) and *Beth Chatto's Woodland Garden* (2002).

JAMES COMPTON trained in horticulture at the Royal Botanic Gardens, Kew, and gained his PhD in botany of *Actaea* from the University of Reading. Having travelled widely, he has plant collections from Argentina, China, Mexico, South Africa, South Korea and Turkey.

James is the author of *Success with Unusual Plants* (1987) and has contributed to *The RHS Dictionary of Gardening*, *European Garden Flora* and several scientific and horticultural papers. A committee member of RHS Floral A, the Advisory Panel on Nomenclature and, most recently, the Horticultural Board of the Royal Horticultural Society, James is also a Fellow of the Linnean Society of London and a Research Fellow at the University of Reading. James acts as botanical advisor to *Gardens Illustrated*.

GARY DUNLOP is a practising architect. He has an enthusiastic interest in plants, with an emphasis on Asiatic, southern hemisphere and woodland species. He has significant collections of many unusual and neglected, as well as common, genera, ranging from South African sun-lovers, through Antipodean alpines, to moisture- and shade-loving plants, mostly from the northern hemisphere.

Gary's interest in gardening developed when he created a half-acre garden from scratch – this soon became too small. He now

gardens informally on a 3.5-acre plot on an exposed hill top in Northern Ireland, which has relatively shallow, light acid soil and natural rock features, and where a surprising diversity of plants thrive, despite the climate.

Gary has published a number of articles on a diverse range of plants. He spends his free time actively researching the genera he has collected.

JENNY HENDY achieved a degree in botany at the University College of North Wales, Bangor. She then joined an expedition to the South American rainforest, where she worked alongside a team of scientists and adventurers trialing a revolutionary method of accessing the canopy using a giant hot air balloon and inflatable pontoon.

Jenny honed her research and writing skills during five years with *Gardening Which?* magazine. She now works as a freelance writer and travels in Britain and abroad, searching out stories about people, plants and gardens. Her enthusiasm for plants and her desire to communicate with gardeners at all levels, has led to many appearances as a guest television presenter. Jenny also lectures, holds a teaching position at one of Britain's most prestigious garden centres and runs a garden design consultancy with a difference – encouraging her clients to become actively involved in all stages of planning, construction and planting.

Jenny is the author of a number of titles, including *Quick and Easy Topiary and Green Sculpture* (1996), *Balconies and Roof Gardens* (1997), *Zen in Your Garden* (2001), and *Garden of the Senses* (2002). She is currently working on her twelfth book.

CHRISTOPHER HOLLIDAY originally worked in the hotel business. In 1988, however, Christopher and his partner, Richard, purchased Charney Well in Grange-over-Sands, South Cumbria, for the panoramic view of Morecambe Bay. The garden, on a steep hillside with no vehicular access, transformed his life. Although he had little gardening experience, he realized that the house, with its sheltered south-east aspect and Gulf Stream influence, was a perfect location for creating an unusual garden. Christopher immersed himself in the world of sub-tropical foliage. A course on garden design in the early 1990s confirmed his change of career to freelance garden designer and writer.

In 1997, Christopher opened his sub-tropical garden for the National Gardens Scheme and, after it appeared on *BBC Gardeners' World* a year later, visitors flocked there. His articles on garden design and exotic and unusual plants, are widely published. Christopher has contributed to the NGS 75th anniversary book, *Making Gardens*, and is the author of *Sharp Gardening*, to be published by Frances Lincoln in 2004.

JOHN HOYLAND is a nurseryman with a life-long passion for plants. Fifteen years ago he gave up a long career in computing and set about building a garden and establishing a nursery (specialising in bulbous and perennial plants) in the foothills of the French Mediterranean Pyrenees. Both the garden and the nursery quickly became a Mecca for French plant enthusiasts.

In 1997 John's roots dragged him back to Britain and, with his partner Nick Downing, he bought Pioneer Nurseries in Letchworth, the world's first Garden City, in Hertfordshire. The nursery was established in 1903 and named after the people who spearheaded the Garden City movement, the Letchworth Pioneers, but had been in decline and was virtually abandoned by the time Nick and John stepped in. They are now working hard to make it a pleasant and fascinating place to visit and to work in. John is interested not only in organic gardening, but also in gardening in the least environmentally damaging way possible.

John contributes regularly to *Gardens Illustrated*, *The Times*, *The Independent* and *The Daily Telegraph*.

After qualifying at the Hertfordshire College of Agriculture and Horticulture, **JIM JERMYN** spent several years in a training programme focusing on growing alpine plants. He worked for ten weeks in the Schachen Garden in the Wetterstein Mountains, Bavaria, and later set up a nursery on the shores of Lake Garda, Italy, where he made many trips into the surrounding mountains to study the endemic flora.

In 1978 Jim took over the well-known Edrom Nurseries in Berwickshire and remained there for 20 years. He exhibited plants at many flower shows throughout the UK and received numerous awards. He has also led many botanical tours to the Dolomites and taken part in one of the Alpine Garden Society's field trips to Japan.

Since 2000 he has been Show Manager of Scotland's Premier Flower Show, Gardening Scotland. He lectures all round the world, as well as writing articles and books. His most recent book is *The Himalayan Garden – Growing Plants from the Roof of the World* (2001). Jim is currently working on a new publication on growing plants native to the European Alps.

KARAN JUNKER has had a passion for plants since childhood. Her husband, Nick, trained as a tree surgeon and together they own and run Junker's Nursery in Somerset. They first bought the site as a green field in 1986 and developed it initially as a wholesale nursery, designed to supply the increasing plant needs of their tree surgery and landscape business. However, to satisfy demand from local garden centres, they soon began to introduce plants that were a little different to the mainstream. They sourced and developed an increasingly exciting range – including acers, tree cornus and daphnes – building a collection of many different species and cultivars.

As the nursery is now well established, Karan is able to spend more time developing display gardens, which double as stock plants. She has also written articles for the *The Garden*, *Gardens Illustrated* and *The Sunday Times*.

NOEL KINGSBURY is well-known as a writer on plants and gardens and is part of a Europe-wide network of gardeners and designers exploring the contemporary 'naturalistic style' and challenging conventional ways of thinking.

With a background in the nursery business, he focuses on plants and their role in garden and landscape design. Primarily interested in the planting of public spaces and involved in promoting sustainable planting in British parks, his largest project to date has been at the Cowley Manor Hotel in Gloucestershire. Further plantings are being developed for parks in Bristol and several other cities as part of Noel's PhD.

Research and worldwide travel are a major part of Noel's work. He believes that seeing plants growing in their natural habitat can tell us about their use in the garden; relating plant ecology to the garden is a central tenet of his writing. He has contributed to a variety of publications and is the author of ten books, including *New Perennial Garden* (1996) and *Natural Gardening in Small Spaces* (2003).

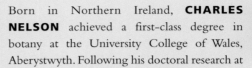

BRIAN MATHEW's career began at The Royal Horticultural Society Garden at Wisley. In 1967 he joined the Royal Botanic Gardens, Kew, where he worked as a botanist for 25 years. Brian has a keen interest in growing plants and using them to the best effect in gardens, and has travelled widely to study bulbous plants in the field, notably in the Middle East and Central Asia.

Brian is the winner of numerous awards, including the Herbert Memorial Medal from the International Bulb Society and the Warburton Trophy from the American Iris Society. For his contribution to horticulture the Royal Horticultural Society has awarded him their highest accolade – the Victoria Medal of Honour.

Brian has lectured widely and written numerous scientific papers, as well as 17 books, which range from authoritative monographs – *The Iris* (1981) – to field guides – *Cyclamen of Turkey* (2001) – and more garden-orientated books – *Growing Bulbs* (1997) and *Bulbs, The Four Seasons* (1998). From 1993 to July 2002, he was the Editor of the prestigious *Curtis's Botanical Magazine*. Brian is also an Honorary Research Fellow of the Royal Botanic Gardens, Kew, and is on the Horticultural Board of the Royal Horticultural Society.

ALASDAIR MOORE is the Assistant Head Gardener at Tresco Abbey Gardens on the Isles of Scilly. As a student, Alasdair worked on a farm in North Yorkshire where he first learnt to appreciate plants. Despite his degree in English Literature, his enthusiasm for gardening led him, in 1990, into a job as an assistant gardener at Queen's Park in London. He completed his studentship at Tresco, trained at The Royal Horticultural Society Garden at Wisley and worked with The National Trust and Marilyn Abbot at West Green House in Hampshire, before returning to Tresco in 1995. In 1997 Alasdair was awarded a Winston Churchill Fellowship to study proteas in South Africa and in 2000 he achieved distinction on the Kew Botanic Garden Management Diploma Course. Alasdair has led a series of garden tours to the French Riviera, Madeira and South Africa.

In addition to gardening, Alasdair is a beekeeper, a heliport fireman, a radio operator, an auxiliary coastguard and, perhaps most importantly, captain of the Tresco Cricket Club.

Born in Northern Ireland, **CHARLES NELSON** achieved a first-class degree in botany at the University College of Wales, Aberystwyth. Following his doctoral research at the Australian National University, Canberra, Charles returned to Ireland and, in 1976, joined the staff of the National Botanic Gardens, Glasnevin, Dublin, as Horticultural Taxonomist.

An acknowledged authority on Irish gardens and plants, Charles was a founding member of the Irish Garden Plant Society and served three terms as its chairman; he was made an Honorary Member in 1996. He has a keen interest in garden history and is President of the Northern Ireland Heritage Gardens Committee.

Charles is a freelance botanist, lecturer and editor. His publications include *An Irish Flower Garden Replanted* (1997), *A Heritage of Beauty: The Garden Plants of Ireland* (2000), which was voted 'Best Reference Book 2001' by the Garden Writers' Guild, and, most recently, *Orchids of Glasnevin* (2003).

Charles regularly leads holiday tours to Crete and Ireland and has travelled on plant-collecting trips to Burma, South Africa and Spain. He now lives in the Fenlands of West Norfolk with his wife, Sue.

MARTYN RIX is a botanist, gardener and traveller with a keen interest in wild flowers. After studying at Trinity College Dublin, Cambridge and the Botanic Garden of Zurich University, he worked as a botanist at The Royal Horticultural Society Garden at Wisley. Martyn's expedition to eastern Turkey in 1965 was the first of many visits to Turkey and Iran to study fritillaries and other bulbs. Plant collecting abroad and growing new hardy species for gardens continue to interest him today.

Martyn is the Editor of *Curtis's Botanical Magazine*, the oldest illustrated plant magazine (first published in 1787), and the author of a number of books, including *The Art of the Botanist* (1981) and, with Roger Phillips, *Bulbs* (1989). His most recent publication is *The Botanic Garden* (2002). In 1999 Martyn was awarded the Gold Veitch Memorial Medal from the Royal Horticultural Society.

For the past 10 years Martyn has been working on a woodland, bog and meadow garden in North Devon, experimenting and developing his ideas on natural planting.

JOE SHARMAN started gardening as a child. At the age of six he was looking after his own plants and small garden. He attended his first plant sale at 19 and, in between college and work on various nurseries, he grew many unusual plants, which he either donated to his local NCCPG group or sold to specialist nurseries.

Joe calls himself a generalist plantsman, specialising in many different areas. Snowdrops, variegated plants and pulmonarias are a particular passion. In 1988 Joe began visiting nurseries on the continent and since then has collected plants in the wild on planthunting trips all over the world. He also seek out plants for National Collection holders. Joe is currently learning about ferns, native grasses and improving his knowledge of native plants.

In 1989 Joe set up Monksilver Nursery to sell the unusual plants he had collected over the years. He has exhibited at the Chelsea Flower Show with the Cambridge NCCPG group and assisted at many other shows. Joe contributes regularly to the local and national gardening press and has given numerous lectures to local garden clubs and the Royal Horticultural Society on a wide range of topics.

ALAN STREET grew up in the Oxfordshire village of Blewbury. After leaving school, he worked at Ratcliffe's in Oxfordshire where he grew orchids under glass. While studying horticulture at Merrist Wood College, Surrey, he made his first important discovery – a bi-generic hybrid x *Halimiocistus wintonensis* 'Merrist Wood Cream'.

As a student, Alan spent a year working at the Pepinieres Croux nursery in France, digging and root-boxing specimen trees for the Paris streets, and six months at the famous Waterer's nursery in Bagshot, Surrey. After college, he moved to Colonel Mars of Haslemere, located at Kingston Bagpuize House in Oxfordshire, a small specialist nursery with an impressive collection of bulbous plants. The business was sold in 1979, renamed Avon Bulbs and relocated to Somerset. Alan works there as nursery and show manager and still finds time to write articles for the gardening press. Alan loves growing and showing plants and has been rewarded by a string of Gold Medals from the Royal Horticultural Society.

JOHN VANDERPLANK spent most of his childhood in Africa, where he developed a keen interest in flora and fauna. Once back in the UK, a practical career in horticulture seemed appropriate, especially as he had already started a small nursery (Greenholm Nursery) while still at school. He enrolled at the Somerset College of Agriculture and Horticulture and studied commercial horticulture for a year.

John's interest in passion flowers developed as the result of a chance conversation with a friend who gave him two unnamed *Passiflora*. Despite reading numerous books he couldn't find a name for them but the more he read the more passion flowers he discovered. Over the next 12 months he acquired a further six or seven *Passiflora* taxa and the following year he exhibited them at the Bristol Flower Show.

Greenholm Nursery has expanded over the years and John now has a successful retail business selling passion flower seeds. His National Collection boasts over 250 *Passiflora*, including approximately 200 different species, and is now acknowledged as the most comprehensive collection of *Passiflora* in the world.

RICHARD WILFORD began his career at the Royal Botanic Gardens, Kew, in 1989. He was initially responsible for the extensive bulb collection in the Alpine Nursery but, after six and a half years, he took charge of the Rock Garden, gaining valuable experience in growing alpines and bulbs in the open. He is currently the Collections Manager, responsible for hardy herbaceous plants, alpines and bulbs. He develops the collections to support Kew's scientific work and to create attractive and informative plantings for the public.

Richard is on the editorial committee and writes for *Curtis's Botanical Magazine*. As well as contributing to *Gardens Illustrated*, he has produced several articles for the Alpine Garden Society and writes a regular column for *Kew*, the magazine for the Friends of the Royal Botanic Gardens, Kew. He is a keen photographer and often takes pictures to illustrate his articles.

Richard gardens at his home in West Sussex, mainly growing herbaceous perennials, while his wife, Kate, prefers to grow a range of fruit and vegetables.

INDEX

Published by BBC Worldwide,
Woodlands, 80 Wood Lane,
London W12 0TT

First published 2003
Text © 2003 John and Jean
Ainsworth, Rosie Atkins,
Rupert Bowlby, Mark Brown,
Beth Chatto, James Compton,
Gary Dunlop, Jenny Hendy,
Christopher Holliday, John
Hoyland, Jim Jermyn, Karan
Junker, Noel Kingsbury, Brian
Mathew, Alasdair Moore,
Charles Nelson, Martyn Rix,
Joe Sharman, Alan Street, John
Vanderplank, Richard Wilford
The moral right of the authors
has been asserted.

All the profiles that appear here
have been previously published
in Gardens Illustrated magazine.

ISBN 0 563 48835 2

All rights reserved. No part of
this book may be reproduced in
any form or by any means
without permission in writing
from the publisher, except by a
reviewer who may quote brief
passages in a review.

Commissioning editor:
Vivien Bowler
Project editor: Sarah Miles
Copy-editor: Deborah Savage
Designer: Andrew Barron
Art director: Sarah Ponder
Production controller:
Kenneth McKay
Jacket art director: Pene Parker

The Gardens Illustrated team:
Hannah Attwell, Samantha
Boddy, Dr James Compton,
Melissa Dring, Clare Foster,
Galiena Hitchman, Heleen van
der Mark, Lisa Richards, Juliet
Roberts, Rae Spencer-Jones,
Claudia Zeff

Set in Bembo and Frutiger
Printed and bound in Singapore
by Tien Wah Press
Colour separations by Radstock
Reproductions Ltd, Midsomer
Norton

BBC Worldwide would like to
thank the following for
permission to reproduce
copyright material. While every
effort has been made to trace
and acknowledge all copyright
holders, we would like to
apologise for any errors or
omissions.

Nicola Browne: 86; Jonathan
Buckley: 12, 61, 90l, 121l; Brian
Carter: 144r; Dee Daneri: 236tr;
Charles Dawes: 234br; Fototek:
235tr; Kate Gadsby: 172, 174,
175, 176l, 176r, 177, 178, 179;
John Glover: 2, 22, 26r, 36, 82,
84, 85l, 96, 100r, 105, 106, 108,
109, 110l, 110r, 112, 113l, 113r,
114, 118, 128, 146, 147t, 151,
164, 168l, 168r, 169, 170;
Garden Picture Library: 14, 16l,
16r, 17, 20, 26l, 28, 32r, 33, 34,
35, 40, 41, 45, 46, 60, 64, 66,
67, 69, 71l, 71r, 72, 74l, 76, 78,
80, 88, 91, 93, 94, 98, 102,
116, 125, 130, 132l (also on
cover), 132r, 137l, 137r, 138,
143, 144r, 147b, 158, 159, 161,
205r, 209, 210r, 218l, 218r;
Jenny Hendy: 167, 171; Harpur
Garden Library: 58l, 62, 87;
C Ireland-Jones: 121r; Jim
Jermyn: 162, 163l, 163r; Andrea
Jones: 235br; Andrew Lawson:
10, 18, 24, 25, 27, 30, 32l, 38,
42l, 43, 44, 59, 74r, 75, 83, 90r,
92, 100l, 101, 103, 104, 117,
119, 120, 122, 124, 126, 127,
133, 140, 148, 150, 206, 212;
Marianne Majerus: 233tr; Brian
Mathew: 142, 144l, 152, 154;
S & O Mathews: 70, 85r, 95;
Clive Nichols: 6, 19, 21;
Joanne O'Brien: 235tl; Photos
Horticultural: 68; Howard Rice:
1, 29, 42r, 77, 129, 135, 136,
153, 155, 211; Howard Sooley:
front cover, 3, 4, 37, 48, 50l,
50r, 51 (also on cover), 52l, 52r,
53, 54, 56, 58r, 63, 156 (also on
cover), 160, 180, 182l, 182r,
183, 184, 185, 186 (also on
cover), 187, 188, 190, 192l,
192c, 192r, 193, 194, 195, 196,
198, 200, 201, 202, 203, 204,
205l, 214, 216, 217, 219, 220,
221; Derek St Romaine
Photography: 79; John
Vanderplank: 9, 208, 210l, 213.